Joys and Sorrows

PHYLLIS WILLMOTT

Joys and Sorrows

Fragments from the Post-war Years

PETER OWEN
London & Chester Springs PA

PETER OWEN PUBLISHERS
73 Kenway Road London SW5 ORE
Peter Owen books are distributed in the USA by
Dufour Editions Inc. Chester Springs PA 19425–0007

First published in Great Britain 1995
© Phyllis Willmott 1995

ISBN 0–7206–0931–3

A catalogue record for this book is available from
the British Library

Printed and made in Great Britain
by Biddles of Guildford and King's Lynn

Contents

The characters in this book are real, but some I have given fictitious names, and sometimes I have changed revealing details.

P.M.W.

1

Finding the Way

It was early December 1946 and the foggy atmosphere and a gentle drizzle reflected on pavements and shone on the faces of passers-by. On such an evening it seemed surprising that Mr Baxter should be standing at the door of his shop, and even more so that he should bellow out across the pavement to me as I got off the bus opposite the row of shops at the top of our road. I'd known Mr Baxter – the manager of the Co-op butcher's shop – since I was a child. With his black cap of greased-down hair, his deathlike pallor and bellicose ways, he had always seemed a bit of a frightening figure to me, and I had probably not exchanged more than a dozen words with him throughout my childhood or, for that matter, since I had become an adult. But it was clear that he now had something to say to me, so I went over to the doorway in which he was standing.

'Good God gal, how are you?' he said, and without waiting for my answer went on: 'You're looking pretty well.' I nodded. 'You've had a bloody rough time, though, haven't you?' I nodded again, more vigorously. It was enough; Mr Baxter had something momentous to communicate, to which I had only to listen. 'Mark my words . . . ask your mother – when you were that ill, when it was touch and go, I said to her, "Gal, you don't want to worry. That girl won't die. THAT-GIRL-WON'T-DIE. If she'd've been going to die, she'd've been bleeding dead already!"'

When Mr Baxter stopped me I was on my way home after being demobbed from the WAAF, and it was the first time our paths had crossed since I had come out of hospital after an emergency admission while at home on a few days' leave. By the time I left the hospital, six months later, two major operations and an attack of jaundice had turned me into a walking skeleton.

Poor Mum. She could never forget that terrible evening when the consultant had warned her I was likely to die; and after I got back home she kept looking at me in that anxious way, brown eyes moist, as if she could hardly believe what she saw – that I had actually survived. For the time being, all the worries I had caused her during my adolescent years, all the quarrels I had provoked by the airs and graces picked up, as she saw it, at the grammar school – all memories of these had vanished, in her gratitude at my just being there.

Convalescent after the first serious illness of my life, I was content for a while to be treated as the invalid Mum clearly thought I was. But within a few weeks her cosseting care 'to build up my strength' and get me back to my normal 'skinny' state of around eight stone began to pall on me. As health and vitality returned I knew – what she was reluctant to accept – that the time had come for me to get on with life again, which meant first of all my returning to the WAAF to get demobilized. Yet, at the same time, the truth was that after so long out of things I was almost as apprehensive about picking up the threads as Mum was on my behalf.

Getting demobbed turned out to be even more unpleasant than I had feared. During my long stay in hospital I had been 'posted' to a new and unknown station, and during my absence my kit had been sent on there and put in store. When in early December 1946 I got to the new station and opened my kitbag I found that not only was everything damp but that my tin of talcum powder had burst inside it and everything was covered with a cloying layer of dirty-white powder.

It was the start to a miserable forty-eight hours, for there was no escaping the regulatory 'arriving' at and 'clearing' from this station I did not know, and would never now be part of. Long before I reached the sick-bay to report to the RAF medical officer I was beginning to feel that Mum had been right, and that I was not nearly as well as I had thought. When I stood in front of the doctor, tears welled up in my eyes as I answered his questions. He looked as if he was not much older than me and, embarrassed by my obvious distress, quickly brought the interview to a close. 'I think the sooner you get home again the better,' he said sympathetically and, feeling as sorry for myself as I did, this brought me even closer to tears.

I set off on the last stage of getting demobbed after a cold and lonely night in a hut full of cheery but unfamiliar WAAFs, among whom I felt a complete outsider. At the end of a long, slow train journey northwards to the dispersal centre in Lancashire I had a bad time convincing a bumptious WAAF corporal that the state of the jumbled and disgusting-looking kit I was handing in was no fault of mine.

Next morning, after another night much like the preceding one, I was on my way back to London. As the train puffed along I remembered how happy I had been working on remote Bomber Command airfields until the war in Europe ended and boredom set in as everything ground slowly down. No wonder that all these months later it seemed as if I had shed being a WAAF, along with the uniform, like an old skin I no longer needed. Whatever lay ahead, I felt that at last I was closer to a new beginning – a feeling that seemed to be confirmed by my brief exchange with Mr Baxter when I returned to the familiar home ground of Lee in south-east London.

I had made up my mind that I was not going back to the kind of boring office life I had formerly known, with its daily round of commuting on crowded rush-hour trains from suburb to City; and I knew that to avoid this fate I had to get the sort of qualifications I did not have. Fortunately, a small service gratuity, added to the savings from my WAAF pay, meant that I could afford to take a little time to decide about future plans.

Until I knew what these were to be, it seemed natural to turn again to Morley College, that mecca for educational self-advancement to which my friend Pluckie had introduced me in the early years of the war when we were still both working as bank clerks in the City. I decided to begin limbering up for whatever my future was to be by taking up ballet classes. I loved ballet, and I convinced myself that this was just the kind of physical activity I needed as a final stage for recovering good health.

At the age of twenty-four I had no illusions that I could have a career as a dancer, but even as an amateur evening-class student I did not last long. I found the dancing enjoyable enough, but it was the pirouettes that defeated me. Try as I did, I could not get the hang of them, and felt I never would once I had noticed the young men who made a point of dawdling past on their way to their own classes on serious subjects like economics, psychology or accountancy. Their amused, bemused or mocking glances proved too embarrassing for me and after a few weeks I gave up. Not that it mattered, for the experience, brief as it was, had served its purpose. It had helped me to realize that the time for drifting was over.

One thing I was sure of from my brush with death was that I was lucky to be alive. It had left me with a sense of gratitude and a vague feeling that I had some sort of debt to repay. It was in that mood that I found my way early in the new year of 1947 to one of the Government's special post-war advice services. This was in Tavistock Square, where I was pleasantly surprised by the courteous manner of the young-ish man who interviewed me. He seemed really concerned to discover what my ideas for my future might be.

As I had grown up with the expectation that working for a living was the norm for everyone over the compulsory school-leaving age of fourteen, I believed that I had already been privileged by being allowed to say on at school until sixteen. For this reason it was not surprising, perhaps, that when the key question came of what I actually had in mind to do, my courage failed me. I could not bring myself to admit that I had begun to dream of becoming a doctor, which would mean my being a student until I was past thirty. 'Well,' I said cautiously, 'I'm not really sure, but I don't want to work in an office, and I'd like to do something really worth-while.' 'You mean like social work?' the youngish man asked. I grasped at the straw: 'Yes. Well, that sort of thing.' Minutes later I was entering the door of a building a few yards further along on the same side of the square.

The young man had telephoned to make an immediate

appointment for me to visit the Institute of Hospital Almoners who, he had told me, were running post-war emergency courses to train almoners – hospital social workers – of whom there was, partly as a result of the war, a great shortage. There I found out that the youngest age for candidates for the special intensive course was twenty-five – the age I would reach by the time the next course began in October. I took away the form, filled it in and sent it off.

It was still very much winter, and the most severe one in Britain since 1894. Not long afterwards, on a bitterly cold day, I went back to Tavistock Square for an interview. Overnight it had snowed heavily again and the pavements were icy under the layer of white. The day had begun with a dilemma over what I should wear. Although during the war the everyday wearing of hats had been more or less abandoned, they were still expected on more formal occasions. And for such a day as this I believed that the hat should ideally be matched to a neat 'costume' plus, possibly, court shoes. I had always found these uncomfortable and, much as Mum favoured such shoes for herself, they invariably changed my normal long-legged stride into what she complained was 'kibbling along'. It was only after much indecision and hesitation that I decided the foul weather gave me an excuse to dress for comfort rather than correctness.

As I walked round the snow-covered Bloomsbury square, getting nearer and nearer to my destination, my confidence in my decision decreased. Had I been right, after all, to believe that wellington boots, my old green waterproof and a brown woollen hood would be seen as showing commendable common sense (much to be desired in an aspirant social worker), not as a rebellious flouting of convention. Confidence plunged further when I found myself facing an interview with half a dozen very upright-looking women, several of whom *were* wearing hats. Concerned as I was by this time that my whole future was about to be decided, when the first question came it seemed as if I had lost the power to speak. It was as if my lips had frozen – not because of the cold but from fear.

'I see that you have recently taken up ballet,' began one of the women. 'What made you do that?' I had to run the tip of my tongue painstakingly right round my lips before I could get out an answer. Haltingly, I managed to explain about my love of ballet and how the classes had helped to restore me to full health. But it was the question that followed which really loosened my tongue. What, one hatted lady asked, had I learnt from being a patient? Appreciative smiles and sympathetic nods spread round as I expanded on hospital life through the eyes of the patient I had been.

It felt like the best news I had had since I heard I had got to the grammar school as an eleven-year-old girl when, the very next day, I had a letter to say that I had been accepted for a place. The letter came from Miss Kit Stewart, organizer of the post-war courses. She had been the one who ushered candidates into the interviews and dealt with their anxious questions afterwards. In contrast to those on the selection panel – women who had seemed at first sight so remote and austere – Miss Stewart had shone in the room like a sunbeam. With her straight golden hair swept back into a bun, she had the face of a Greek goddess. She was tall, slightly stooped and slim, but even more remarkable than her looks was her manner. She exuded a loving concern that was unbelievably charming, and yet at the same time utterly convincing. Equally extraordinary was her way of speaking. To almost every other word she gave an emphasis that was excessive, but also mesmerizingly warm and sincere.

By the time I next met Kit Stewart I had taken on a temporary job with the British Red Cross. It had sounded interesting, but turned out to be merely the filing of endless reports sent back from devastated Europe on the welfare work with refugees and displaced persons – the very kind of work I should have liked to do myself, if I'd had the right qualifications. 'My *dear*,' said Kit, 'we *must* get you more *suit*able temporary work.' And no doubt responding to my anxious look she added, 'But don't *worry*, darling – we shall find *some*thing.'

In the meanwhile she suggested voluntary work in Bermondsey where she had a long-standing connection with a settlement started in 1887 by Christian society ladies intent on 'spiritually awakening and widening the horizens' of young factory girls. Things had moved on a little since 1887, when public houses were the main leisure centres in most streets, and many other schemes and activities in Bermondsey had developed through the settlement. A new one just then in need of volunteers was 'the children's flat'. An undesirable and minuscule dwelling on the ground floor of a bleak block of buildings in Barnham Street, it was to be a place where younger children could come after school to enjoy painting and making and doing things that they couldn't do in their overcrowded homes or out on the streets.

In charge of the children's flat was an earnest worker named Mary Wylmington. She was perhaps thirty, a pretty, blue-eyed brunette who had grown up in a country rectory and now, like a missionary in a savage land, was intent on converting these slum-dwelling children, not so much to Christianity as to the cultural values of her class. She was an admirable, sweet-natured, if slightly smug, young woman, still with the air of the privileged, well-brought-up little girl she had been. There was also a faint aura of sadness about her which, probably quite wrongly, I imagined suggested some unhappy romance. Before letting me loose on the children she made clear that 'the flat belongs to the children and they must use it as they wish', but she added solemnly that at the same time we must 'help the children to realize their responsibility for it and the others who use it'. In general parents were discouraged from entering the flat, let alone staying there (not that any showed signs of wanting to), and it was made quite clear that Mary was boss – or, as she preferred to call it, 'leader'.

Barnham Street was only a short walk from London Bridge Station down Tooley Street. Across the bridge was the City, whose tall buildings and winding streets, despite the ravages of the Blitz, had a prosperous staidness. On this, the south bank of the river, I discovered a different world. In a way, the endless streets of little houses were much like those in which I had grown up in south-east London but without their front gardens and air of respectability. In Bermondsey, they were interspersed with tall Victorian 'buildings', and the terraced cottages opened straight on to the streets and were grimy and dilapidated, and the air was far from fresh.

I noticed one evening walking along Tooley Street that there were many busily noisy warehouses and factories, each of which had a smell of its own. For a few yards a strong smell of toffee dominated. Further on, it was the pungent smell of curing leather. Strongest of all was the heavy odour of fermenting hops. Sometimes vying with each other, sometimes mingling, the smells gave an overwhelming effect of a heavy, slightly repugnant – and to me specifically Bermondsey – odour. As for the Barnham Street buildings, I soon came to recognize that their dank and musty smell, by no means a unique one at the time, was that of slum dwellings.

In the shadow of blackened railway arches, treeless and skyless, the asphalt courtyards between the blocks of looming red brick were the dreary playgrounds for the children. Stone stairways led to the flats, two on each side of a landing with one shared lavatory set between them. The children's flat, like all the others, had two small rooms. The front door opened on to the first room, which was about twelve feet square, and this in turn opened on to the second, which was even smaller. Being on the ground floor of one of the eight-storey 'buildings' the rooms in the children's flat were especially dark. In these hardly inspiring surroundings, I tried with Mary and other volunteers to 'widen the horizons' of the children who, it must be said, flocked in to enjoy the opportunities the flat provided, limited though they were.

Before long, under the influence of Mary's missionary zeal, I was drawn into other things. We took the Barnham Street children for an outing to the 'beach' beside the Tower of London, which, incredibly, they had never visited before and regarded as an exciting adventure. I was sent out collecting for Alexandra Rose Day, and on another occasion was persuaded to attend a meeting for volunteers which took place in an old and dirty hall where there was no water to make tea, and the sound refused to work for the film we were to see. It was replaced by a rather long, impromptu 'talk' by a worker who probably lived in the best part of Kensington but expounded on life in slum Bermondsey with impressive confidence.

I knew I lacked this kind of confidence on the sunny day that inspired Mary to suggest we should take tea to old people sitting out on the benches in a nearby square. Trekking across the busy main road lugging a huge full teapot, milk, sugar and biscuits, plus white china cups and saucers, seemed a pretty eccentric thing to be doing. My fellow-volunteer caught me laughing and asked what was amusing me. I did not like to say that, really, I was disconcerted by the expressions on the faces of the people in the square as we bore down on them – some bemused, others politely tolerant.

Inclined to believe as I did that this was a kind of philanthropy that belonged to the past and not to the bright new post-war war world for which Britain was now striving, nevertheless I did not doubt that my experience of charitable work in Bermondsey was a necessary and valuable preparation for my new career.

2

Marking Time

Within a few weeks Kit Stewart had found something better for me than filing work for the British Red Cross. She sent me along to see Miss Betty Read, chief lady almoner at the prestigious St Thomas's Hospital. Miss Read explained that she and the sister of the children's ward were looking for someone who would play with the children in a way that the nursing staff had no time to do. The idea was to give the children a bit more personal attention and so keep them happily occupied while they were confined to cot, bed and ward – which at that time many patients were for weeks or months. There was no money, Miss Read explained, for a permanent appointment, but charitable funds had been found to pay someone for a few weeks to try out the scheme.

As we walked along the great arched covered way, which was like a busy highway through the heart of the enormous Victorian building, it seemed as if the spirit of Florence Nightingale still lived. In their 'Nightingale' style uniforms the young nurses looked wonderfully pretty – almost bridelike, I thought, with their caps of delicately spotted white net standing high on the hidden wire frames.

At Lilian Ward, Miss Read introduced me to Sister. Her air of dignity and authority was awesome. Like all the sisters she wore a long-sleeved dress of navy poplin under a crisp white apron, and a starched white bonnet trimmed with lace, and with strings which tied in a bow under the chin.

The children's ward, over which Sister Lovely – for that was her charming name – reigned, was a large, high-ceilinged rectangular room on the first or second floor. The walls were decorated with beautiful – but, as I saw them then, old-fashioned – tiles depicting nursery rhymes, and large rocking-horses and other Victorian toys of a kind few of the sick children of Lambeth could ever have seen, let alone have had to play with.

Sister Lovely was, like many women of her class and generation, wholly dedicated to her work. She had created an atmosphere in Lilian Ward of calmness and care, combined with disciplined efficiency. When babes or frightened, homesick toddlers sobbed, which of course they did, her crisp command would ring out: 'Stop that child crying!' It was a frightening command to the young nurses, and also to me, as it was not always easily fulfilled.

There was a rumour that no one came to nurse at St Thomas's unless their father was a brigadier, an admiral or a Harley Street consultant, and there was no doubt that Sister Lovely was what no one then had any hesitation to call a 'lady'. She was, I suppose, in her late thirties or early forties – old enough to be thought of by me as past marrying. Yet unmarried and childless though she was, Sister Lovely was an expert on young children. She would gather junior staff round her in a corner of the ward and give impromptu and absorbing little lectures, and at such times her love of children and her wisdom seemed to cast a spell of peaceful quietness over the whole ward.

One day she talked about the importance of intuition. On countless occasions, she told us, she had rushed back to the ward at a time of emergency, drawn by no message other than this invisible power. Given her devotion to Lilian Ward, this was not hard to believe. She believed that all children were born with this power, but that most lost it before reaching adulthood because it needed to be 'spiritually cultivated'. Her long experience with her small patients had also taught her much, not only about their ways but those of their parents, the majority of whom came from the surrounding streets of Lambeth. She had a fund of Lambeth anecdotes, like that of the little girl she overhead telling her doll, 'Go to sleep like a good baby, then I'll take you up the pub for a drink'.

At first, on Lilian Ward, I was almost as frightened as the homesick toddlers, and not at all confident that I could succeed in distracting them, let alone keep them happily occupied. My big fear was that Sister's command – 'Stop that child crying!' – might be aimed at me, as it soon was, but my fear abated once I realized that what underlay the command was concern, not anger. A benevolent despot, Sister Lovely exuded a detached compassion. On sunny days she would order doors to be opened, and children, cots, beds and toys to be moved out on to the large balcony overlooking the Thames. Across the river were the neo-Gothic building and multi-spires of the House of Commons. Below, the noise and bustle of river traffic mingled with that of children well enough to play out of bed, who would be running or pushing toys round the tubs of flowers dotted about on the asphalted roof-top.

Few days were wholly happy. Serious illness and the threat of death were always present, which was disturbing and sad to recognize, alongside the beauty and bloom of the children. It was upsetting when bright, curly-blonde little Valerie who was suffering from nephritis held up her arms to me and sobbed 'Mummy!', and even more so when Sister told me that a small boy, quiet in his cot and looking like an angel, had cancer and was dying.

On the day my short stay came to an end, Sister Lovely invited me across the corridor outside Lilian Ward to take tea with her in her 'sitting-room'. I was surprised on entering to find that this is exactly what it was – a large, comfortably furnished room in which I was to be served tea, brought in on a silver tray by staff. Making polite conversation, Sister poured tea into cups of delicate china and cut me a slice of a home-made cake. I knew then that I had fallen in love with this great hospital and wished I could have become as much a part of it as Sister Lovely. I left at the end of July with regret, hoping that some day I might return.

It was now just over a year since the war in Europe had ended, and my elder brother Wal (who had been in the Bay of Biscay on his way to the Far East on VE Day) and my younger brother Joe (who had been sent to Malta) were, like me, back home after demobilization. Mum had been longing for the return of her 'boys', eager to revert to her ideal of normal life at the hub of a her household of husband, daughter and two sons. Her nightmare fear – that the 'boys' might be killed, as two of her brothers had been in the First World War – was over. What she had not foreseen was that far from losing members of the family by the time the war was over, she was to gain some.

When the war began in 1939 we had shared the same house with Gran and Grandad and my two cousins, Pete and Ken, who had lived with Gran and Grandad since they were orphaned as small boys. The bombs of the Blitz changed that, and Gran and Grandad had had to move to a flat, while Dad had found us another house in a street nearby so that (much to her delight) Mum no longer had to share with her mother-in-law. It was a good move for Dad too, because a large builder's yard behind the house (and approached by an entrance alongside it) could be rented with it. It was what Dad, as a jobbing builder, could only dream of during all the hard, depressing years of the thirties, until the Blitz brought more than enough work to satisfy even his appetite for it.

By the end of the war, uprooted and worn down by the destruction of the way of life they had formerly thrived on and enjoyed, Gran and Grandad were dead. It meant that when my cousin Pete (who had been in Greece with the Royal Fusiliers) and his younger brother Ken (who was in the Fleet Air Arm somewhere in England) were demobilized, they had no home to go to. Except that it seemed natural to everyone that they should move in again with us.

With a household, including Dad, of five adult men and one undomesticated daughter to cater for, at a time when food rationing, far from coming to an end, had worsened, Mum found that her life was in some ways harder than it had been during the war. It might have been easier if she had found in me the supportive and companionable daughter she needed and, against past evidence, still hoped I might become. On the contrary, I was soon doing my best to act more like a lodger than a dutiful daughter. The fact was that, no longer in need of Mum's cosseting care, I missed the freedom of the life I had enjoyed in the WAAF, and the sense of independence I felt I had lost. 'It's ridiculous,' I scribbled furiously in my diary, 'to be forced to live like a

schoolgirl at the age of twenty-four. The war pulled me out
of Lee, and now I must make my own road. There is no
doubt in my mind that I must get [borrowing freely from
Virginia Woolf's book, which was one of my Bibles], "a room
of my own".' By the time my spell on Lilian Ward came to
an end, I had a makeshift answer to the problem. I had
found another job.

It was not Kit Stewart who had put me on to it this time,
but one of my ex-WAAF friends who, like me and so many
others then, were waiting to take up a course for a new
career and was meanwhile doing temporary work. She told
me how to apply for what she was doing, which was work as
a relief warden in hostels for Land Army girls in Surrey. Britain's
desperate food shortages and the dearth of agricultural labour
had led the post-war government to introduce Volunteer
Agricultural Camps. These were proving popular as working
holidays for many people from all walks of life, but there
were still many girls in the Land Army who had largely replaced male agricultural workers during the war. In Surrey,
these girls were employed by the County Agricultural Executive
Committee and lived in hostels from which they were taken
out each day in lorries to work wherever they were needed.
The job of the warden of a hostel was to supervise the housekeeping staff and the general welfare of the girls.

I was not at all equipped for this new job. I had no experience of supervising anyone, and certainly not of being in
charge of a cook, kitchen staff and cleaners as well. I had
virtually no experience of cooking and running a home, let
alone a hostel, and I was almost totally ignorant about ration
books and rationing, first, because Mum had taken charge of
all that at home and, secondly, because in the WAAF my
ration books were handed over except when I was on leave.

Despite these limitations on my part, I made my way happily in mid-July to my first post at West Hall, a large Victorian
country house not far from Byfleet, where I was to learn the
ropes as the assistant to the warden, Mrs Barnett, a thin,
colourless young woman who knew her job and clearly did
not need help from me. She had a huge office in what must
have been a former drawing-room, and there I tried to learn
the mysteries of rations and ration books. Fortunately, be-

cause she did not need my help, my ignorance was either not noticed or not something that troubled her much. In fact, her main idea seemed to be to keep me out of the way, and she did this by giving me an office of my own. In the elegant gloom of its oak-panelled walls, I sat in splendid solitude with nothing much to do most of the time. I was also given a bed-sitting-room, on the ground floor facing the gardens. Barely furnished though it was, with its high, decorated ceiling it was altogether grand. A great bay window, overhung with the fronds of an ancient wisteria, looked out on to vast lawns which, dotted with well-spaced mature trees, swept down to a river bank. At night, with owls hooting, and no one else very near, it was a bit spooky; but in the daytime it seemed like a dream come true – my first 'room of my own'.

Although I was at first very thrilled with what seemed to be such a cushy job in such lovely surroundings, in the short time I was there I was never entirely at ease. One of the jobs that Mrs Barnett did allow me to do was to make up the order for food and household goods in co-operation with Mrs Case, the cook, a dumpy little woman of sixty with an explosive temper. It was harder to conceal my ignorance from her of the everyday facts about rationing and household management; but it soon became clear that she would ignore my weakness if I did hers, of minor fiddles with the rations. On alternate mornings Mary or Ivy from the kitchen staff brought me breakfast in bed, but on the other mornings I had to get up at six o'clock to help serve the girls their breakfast before they set off for the fields and *their* very hard day's work.

The girls seemed to me much younger than I was, although the difference was not great in years. In the chill of the morning they would, after their breakfast, pile cheerfully into the lorry, radiating vitality, their bright faces shining with colour and health. Most had their hair tied back under bright-coloured scarves or turbans, which contrasted oddly with their heavy brown boots and thick khaki dungarees or long socks with breeches. They were nice girls, but it was made clear by Mrs Barnett that staff and girls were not expected to become too friendly.

For a large part of the day, once the girls had left, and as

Mrs Barnett stayed mostly in her office and the kitchen staff lived in some kind of intensely emotional and often quarrelsome whirl of their own, it was a lonely life. Idling in my grand room, or wandering round the gardens, I could not help thinking that these peaceful and beautiful surroundings would be a perfect setting for a new and exciting romance, but there was little hope of that. Apart from wordless flirtation with the handsome German prisoners of war who worked in nearby fields, there was only the old gardener, Mr Cooper, whose main topic of conversation was of the halcyon pre-war days at West Hall, when he was one of an outside staff of sixteen and the garden was 'the showplace of Surrey'.

One good thing was that, now that I had got away from home, my discontent with it diminished, as did the mutual irritation that had begun to build up again between me and Mum. I began to think fondly of her, and of the hard time she had had in the war. There was so much room at West Hall that staff could invite guests to stay, and I soon decided that I would persuade Mum to come down for the August Bank Holiday weekend (which at that time was at the beginning of the month). It worked out well. As I had noticed in the past, there was something of the actress in Mum. She seemed able to adapt herself to her surroundings and take on whatever new role she felt appropriate for them, and the part she had decided to play at West Hall was the amiable, well-mannered and gracious lady. Thoroughly enjoying herself, she smiled warmly at the girls, who responded with far more friendliness than they had to me. She impressed the staff with her genteel manners and, swapping childhood experiences of country life, immediately charmed Mr Cooper. When I took her out on the river in the punt that belonged to the house she would not take off her hat but sprawled out in a relaxed pose, managing to combine her normal bright-eyed curiosity about people with a smug 'Look at me!' air whenever others in punts or on the towpath passed by.

After only a few weeks at West Hall, the order came through from 'County' that I was to move to another hostel a few miles away. It turned out to be a delightful rambling house of ancient red brick whose walls were overgrown with sweet-smelling honeysuckle and climbing roses. After the atmosphere at West hall – which, because of the tensions amongst the staff, could change so unpredictably from cold to hot – South Lodge seemed different but as beautiful, and far more peaceful.

It was a much smaller hostel than West Hall and here I was to be the warden in charge. I soon found that I was not only going to have to mix more with both staff and girls, but was expected to give a hand to Mrs Power, the cook, when she wanted it. Mrs Power did not live in, but as I arrived in the daytime it was she who showed me to the light and comfortable ground-floor room, again at the front of the house, which was to be my sitting-room, bedroom and office. It opened on to the spacious hall which had a red-tiled floor and a tall window rising up the full height of the house to light the oak stairway. From my window I could look out on to the high wrought-iron gate that led up to the porch and front door, normally used only by strangers or special guests. Girls and staff came in through what had no doubt formerly been the tradesmen's entrance near the dining-room and kitchen at the back of the house.

A motherly figure who liked her kitchen to be as full of people as the tables were with her food, cook had me podding peas, making up lunch-packs and icing her slab cakes almost as soon as I had arrived. After the strangely isolated days at West Hall it was good to be useful and I enjoyed it – especially putting the pink and white icing on the cake. The problem was that cook did not seem to believe that I was in charge. As she saw it, her job was not only to cook but to run the hostel in the daytime, and mine was to take over when she was not there. Although most of the time she was like a good-humoured and indulgent mother, when she turned on – as she sometimes did – her bossiest manner, both staff and girls jumped to do her bidding. In their view, too, *she* was boss, and I was her substitute – someone, in other words, the girls felt mostly free to ignore.

At the end of their hard days in the fields, after the girls came back, they washed, showered or bathed, and ate their supper. Full of life and vigour, made up and dressed up, their idea of a good evening was then to make for the nearby pub and flirt and drink away the evening. They were supposed to be indoors again by 10 p.m. and it was my job to see that they were. I tried sympathetic understanding, I tried reasoning – 'I know it's hard, but you must get your sleep, and I must do my job.' Nothing worked. I suppose I was trying, but failing, to become a sort of good-natured head girl. As I sat in my room waiting for the girls to return, my exasperation grew. Uneasily listening for their noisy arrival, I was struck by the irony that, here was I, hardly older than they were yet forced to play the improbable role of disapproving, fun-spoiling parent!

I found the solution accidentally and unexpectedly after the local police constable arrived at the door one evening before the girls got back. He had come, he said, to discuss complaints in the village about the wild behaviour of some of the girls. No one wanted trouble, he explained, and the girls were generally liked and appreciated for the hard work they did, but it was thought that it was time someone in authority at the hostel (like me!) 'had a word with them'. With as much outward confidence as I could muster, and none at all inwardly, I assured the policeman I would do something.

That night the girls were later than ever, and long before they came noisily in I had plenty of time to grow more and more indignant. By the time I heard them stumbling and giggling in the dark on their way to the back entrance I had taken up a position (metaphorically arms akimbo) at the foot of the stairs. I was in a red rage of fury such as I had never known, but which from the look on their faces they recognized instantly. To my astonishment as much as theirs, I heard myself uncontrollably, angrily, bitterly complaining of their behaviour; of the disgrace of having the policeman complaining; of the poor light it threw on the hostel (I had the sense not to add 'and me'); that I was not going to stand such behaviour any longer, and would be reporting to County staff if things didn't improve. By the end of this outburst, I was shaking, the girls were subdued and, as soon as they could, escaped upstairs to bed.

From that night on my troubles were over. For, strangely,

although I have never believed that anger is a good way to exert authority, I had no doubt it was this which had convinced the girls that – at least in the absence of Mrs Power – they had to recognize mine.

I did not have long to enjoy my new-found authority because my three months' contract was almost over. A few weeks later I was back home in south-east London, but happy in the prospect of what lay ahead.

3
Budding Career

Apart from the weather, the summer of 1947 had not been a good one for the country and the cost of the victory celebrated two years earlier was pressing in. It was not only that rationing was still there; it was being widened with a new round of 'austerity' cuts and, while I was enjoying being hostess to Mum at West Hall, the Prime Minister – Mr Attlee – was warning Parliament that the nation was facing a future of 'peril and anxiety'. By the end of the summer the country's financial crisis had led to further cuts in rations, restrictions on petrol for private cars and the banning of foreign holidays.

Although cuts in rations and petrol were of little concern to me (apart from my having to listen to Mum's grumbles about the one, and Wal's about the other), my feelings about a travel ban were more complicated. Since before leaving school at the age of sixteen I had longed to travel. At first, lack of funds had stopped me and later, because of the war, I had had to abandon dreams of discovering the magic world of 'abroad' that I had heard about in geography lessons at school and read about in books galore. Yet although as soon as the war was over these dreams had revived, when the ban on travel was announced I found that I was more relieved than dismayed because I knew that I could now stop hoarding my small savings so carefully and spend a bit on buying new clothes. I 'splashed out' by buying a gaberdine suit of emerald green, very plainly cut, with a straight skirt and the square shoulders then still fashionable – despite Dior's 'new look' – because of clothes rationing.

The new suit was put into use when, in some trepidation, I went to the 'eve of course' party in the last week of September. As I walked through the squares of Bloomsbury, falling leaves in marbled patterns of orange and green now lay on the grass and blew along pavements. The plane trees had changed their dress as much as I had mine, it seemed, since my earlier visits in snow-bound February. When I arrived at the reception in Tavistock Square, the only person I knew in the crowded room was Kit Stewart who, gracious as ever, took me across to join one of the groups. The fifty or so women – plus one or two men – had set off, as such occasions do, a buzz of talking. Most of those present were women who were starting a new career after wartime experience in the forces or other war work. Most were in their late twenties or thirties.

The intensive training course on which we were all about to embark had been devised to increase as rapidly as possible the number of hospital social workers, just as with teachers and other professions at the time. As the Ministry of Health, the Ministry of Labour and the British Medical Association pointed out, not only would more hospital social workers be needed to make good the shortages the war years had caused and to help in rehabilitating the war wounded and sick, but to meet the demands of the new National Health Service. The need to increase numbers quickly meant condensing into one year what was normally a three-year training (a two-year diploma course at university, followed by one-year professional training).

At the end of September I started on the fourth of the five 'post-war emergency courses' that were to add 272 hospital social workers to what was then a quite small profession. With the huge influx of students everywhere at the time, lectures and tutorials had to be held in makeshift and often cramped premises wherever they could be found in Bloomsbury. For me and my fellow-students this proved to be sometimes in back rooms of the Society of Friends' headquarters in Euston Road, sometimes in Tavistock House and, at others, in the historic arts and crafts building of the Mary Ward settlement in Tavistock Place. I knew Bloomsbury as the home of the British Museum, and of Virginia Woolf and the artistic life of the kind I had read about and envied. Now, to my delight, I was introduced to its colleges and libraries.

I learnt that Monday, Tuesday and Thursday of each week in the first term would be taken up with lectures, discussions and tutorials, Wednesday spent on visits to clinics, old people's homes, factories, residential schools and similar suitably educational venues, and Friday would be for private study and essay writing. As I did not have to leave the house until nine o'clock in the morning to arrive in time for the first lecture at 10 or 10.30 a.m., it seemed to me a pretty gentle start to the day. And as for that one day a week for private study, with mixed admiration and exasperation Mum and Dad decided that, once again, their daughter had managed to 'fall on her feet'.

By this time summer was truly over, and on some days as I made my way through the squares winter seemed to be hinting its arrival. In the morning, a bluish mist would be trying to defeat the sun rising behind the trees, dramatizing the looming buildings around. There was still plenty of evidence of the Blitz because of the bomb-sites, although many were now overgrown with wild blooms like buddleia and foxgloves, as well as garden refugees which had somehow survived and flourished untended.

Although this new turn in my life seemed to me wonderfully stimulating, my attempts to persuade Mum of the fascination of lectures on social services, ethics, psychology and social structure proved useless. She showed more interest in hearing about the visits, the first of which was to the day nursery of the Kodak factory. I arrived home after it full of amazement at the self-possession and independence of the three-year-olds I had seen there. To my surprise, at the end of my enthusiastic account Mum remarked that she had often wondered if what she called my 'do-as-you-please attitude' had arisen because she had sent me to kindergarten on the day after I turned three. With my newly acquired knowledge of the environment versus genetic debate, I thought it more likely that the latter might have been the most important influence. Although when I put this to Mum she said nothing, from her pursed-up mouth and the fixed stare in her brown eyes I knew that she was not convinced.

For me, both visits and lectures were sometimes so exciting that I could not get to sleep at night thinking about them. After a visit to a boarding-school for blind girls I worried about how they would fit into the real world when they left, whether in such surroundings lesbianism was likely to be encouraged, and why their prospects of marriage were less good than for blind boys. A lecture by Professor Marshall on social structure had me bothered about the conditions required for optimum freedom in society. After Dr Wilson's psychology lecture on early infancy, in which he stressed that one year in a baby's life 'is a very long time', I was left wondering, first, whether 'time in hours and years is really a very adequate measure' – but then doubted the relevance of such a thought.

Reading-lists too led to new discoveries – and the books in them to yet more. Reading Beatrice Webb's *My Appren-ticeship* I was so impressed by her quotation from another book entitled *Martyrdom of Man* that, emulating her, I stu-diously copied it out: 'Mankind will emigrate into space and will cross airless Saharas. . . . The earth will become a Holy Land visited by pilgrims. . . . They will become themselves architects of systems, manufacturers of worlds. Man will then be perfect; he will be a Creator; he will therefore be what the vulgar worship as God.' Even though 'mankind' has as yet made little progress towards fulfilling all this prophecy, at least the first step – space travel – has been achieved. In 1947 this too seemed absolute fantasy.

Thinking about the Webbs was perhaps more in my mind at this time because, soon after becoming a student, I had noticed an obituary of Sidney Webb while browsing through Dad's newspaper, the *Daily Herald*. I had barely known of the existence of either when Beatrice had died four years earlier, and I had known nothing at all about their unique partnership. I was dismayed at my ignorance, but at the same time delighted at my new state of enlightenment. The Webbs had made me realize that there could be perhaps a form of marriage which was a beginning and not, as I had always feared, the end of life. Not that I could see any prospect of this kind of marriage, or of any other kind, for me at this time.

*

One thing I had learnt was that that, with or without marriage, with or without the passion and romance I had found
– and lost – several times during the war years, much of the
joy in life came from just plain friendship. Despite the dis-
ruptions of war, the bonds with some old friends had en-
dured. There was Meg, whose wartime career as a VAD had
never taken her out of London, and who had with relief
given up nursing as soon as she could to embark on a social
science diploma at Bedford College. It was with Meg that I
made my way one evening in November to the press gallery
of St Pancras Town Hall in Euston Road to see a council
meeting. As Meg said, it was a good idea to find out what
happened in practice in local government, in order to compare it with the lectures we were both having on what local
government was supposed to be doing. My first reaction
was of indignation at the order to stand to attention as the
mace was brought in, but I was more favourably impressed
with the actual proceedings – the mixture of tradition, bickering, application to order papers and recurrent humour. A
Communist delegation was being heard, and gave voice to
its violent opposition to a proposed cut in the building pro-
gramme. At a time when in the United States the first signs
of anti-Communist investigations were being raised, and General
de Gaulle was waging war with Communists in France, I was
deeply impressed that here 'in funny old England' the delegation had at least been allowed to have a say, long-winded
and boring though it seemed.

Another close friend was Pluckie, whom I'd got to know
at the beginning of the war when we started work at about
the same time as clerks in a bank in Bishopsgate. A committed
pacifist, when we had been called up she had rejected the
route I had taken into the forces and joined the Women's
Timber Corps of the Land Army. As a result, she had had a
much harder time, cutting down trees and making pit-props
and charcoal in forests in the West Country, sometimes in
weather so bitter and conditions so primitive that buckets of
ice had to be broken with an axe before tea could be made.
She had, however, been able to get back earlier to civilian
life, and having quickly qualified as a teacher was already
launched on her new career at a primary school in the East

End. When we next met, she was overwhelmed and exhausted by the early shocks of teaching at a primary school in tough, impoverished and war-battered Whitechapel. As always, we had lots to say to each other about the new directions our lives were taking. Since in her case, she said, she badly needed 'to get away from things', we went to see and wonder at a marvellous exhibition of Van Goghs, and before parting arranged to meet again early in the new year to go to one of the 'Christmas Proms' at the Albert Hall.

As well as the company of old friends there was always, too, the pleasure of new ones like Rose, the daughter of Mrs Green, the Bermondsey widow in the bed next to mine during my long stay in hospital who I had watched die painfully, but uncomplainingly, of cancer. Like me, Rose was in her early twenties, but she was already married. She had met her husband, Harry, a divorced man in his forties, at the fur factory in Bermondsey where he was the company director and she his secretary. An educated man of high intelligence, sophisticated, fatherly and charming, Harry offered Rose the comfort that her life had lacked and that her mother's death had further undermined.

With her fair skin, thin fluffy hair and nervous, almost twitchy, movements there was something appealingly fragile about Rose. It was a vulnerability that was, paradoxically, further emphasized when she wore the expensive fur coat Harry had chosen for her. After they married, Rose, obedient to Harry's wishes, gave up working at the factory and, like the lady of leisure she had become, took to voluntary work. She was pleased, indeed proud, that Harry could afford to buy her not just a fur coat but a house in the suburbs. She was glad to escape from the back streets of Bermondsey where she had grown up. I envied her the fur coat, but not the life of a suburban housewife.

Although happy enough to accept occasional invitations to her new home (mainly because of Harry's erudite expositions on esoteric subjects such as the importance of semantics to future society), I preferred to meet Rose when she joined me in Bermondsey to do voluntary work, which that December included taking a party of thirty children to the circus. We went by coach to some vast building – perhaps it was Wembley – and, for a reason I've forgotten, found that we had to leave before the show ended. For once I was far more nervous and uncertain than Rose was when we had to insist it was time to go. It was she who undermined the threatened rebellion of the children by a counter-threat: that we would leave without them if they did not come. It was I who feared her bluff would be called – that these sharp, streetwise kids might realize we could hardly manhandle them from their seats if all thirty of them held out! To my relief, grumbling and protesting they gave in as Rose, to my surprise, had never doubted they would.

4

High and Low Life

At the end of my first term as a student I put aside study and essays to join in the preparations at home for Christmas – the first time since the war that the family would be all together again. I put up the decorations and iced the cake, sent off my Christmas cards, bought my presents and enjoyed what Mum dismissively but quite good-humouredly called my 'gadding about'. This included going up to the centre of London to meet Ann Horton, a new friend (and fellow-student) from the course.

Ann was a year or two older than I was. She had bitten-down nails, a funny, puggish face with protuberant eyes, and mousy hair. But, with her long legs, neat ankles and a good figure, she was attractive. Like most of my fellow-students, she was from the sort of background where early independence had been encouraged (or forced) by a boarding-school education – in her case also a Catholic one – and she had the confident manner of her class.

On one occasion she and I and another student called Ruth were having lunch together in a restaurant that was a bit above our normal student level of smartness. We were at the coffee stage when Ruth (whose boarding-school had been Roedean) looked at her cup and said 'Oh dear!'. She had found that the edge of her cup was smeared with the red lipstick of a previous customer. 'It's *disgusting*!' Ann exclaimed, and she looked round angrily for the waiter. Fearing a scene, I was relieved to hear Ruth say quietly, when the waiter came over: 'I am *so* sorry, but I am afraid my cup is a trifle stained.' It was a lesson, I realized, on the subtle social class differences between us. I knew that I would have just turned the cup round and drunk out of the other side rather than make a fuss, that Ann would have been rude and that only Ruth, of the three of us, was what Mum would have called 'a real lady'. Perhaps this was also why Ruth seemed to keep her distance from us. She was always very pleasant and agreeable, but I formed the impression that her social circle was that of the parental home in the country, to which she returned at weekends.

In contrast, Ann and I were soon on intimate terms. Ann's story put a new perspective on my own wartime romances, from which I had emerged saddened and wiser but not struck down by tragedy as Ann had been. I found out that during the war she had been a VAD, that she had met and married a young doctor by whom she was pregnant by the time he was sent overseas with the Army. Some time later a telegram had come to say he was wounded. Worse was to follow: she learnt he had died at the battle for Monte Cassino. Soon after the news reached Ann she had a miscarriage. Widowed, her hopes of motherhood cruelly dashed, and still mourning her loss, she hoped by turning to a career in social work to find new meaning in life.

Ann was a committed Catholic but although, she said, this gave her some sort of consolation, it had not helped her to accept what had happened. One Monday morning in our first term she arrived looking on edge and unhappy. In the coffee-break between lectures she told me she had stayed that weekend with friends, a young married couple. Before the war had split them all up Ann and her husband had seen a lot of this couple (the two men in the foursome had been fellow-students at medical school), and since being widowed the couple had done all they could to support and help her.

The two had moved to the country just after the birth of their first baby, and the weekend had been Ann's first visit to their new home. She had arrived on Saturday afternoon, admired the baby and had a happy evening; but after going up to bed she found she could not get to sleep because of an increasing sense of breathlessness. On the second night it was worse. The whole household had been disturbed and her friends had rushed into her room to find out what was wrong. It was a severe attack of asthma – the first she had ever had.

Although it owed a lot to the psychiatric insights we were

in process of acquiring from our lectures, Ann's conclusion that it was envy of the couple's happiness and anger at what she had lost that had caused the attack seemed to me to be right. And so did her decision that she must avoid overnight visits to these friends for a while. Ann had a wide social circle, including other friends she knew from her husband's old rugby club. When we met in the vacation, she told me she had been invited by some of this group to a New Year's Eve dinner-dance at the Strand Palace Hotel, and that she had been asked to find another girl to make up the party. Would I like to go?

I was delighted, and on New Year's Eve I got the train from Lee to Charing Cross dressed for the occasion in the only suitable garment I had. It was ankle-length, and of green watered taffeta, with ruched frilling round the scooped neckline and its short puffed sleeves. It was not new when I bought it, and I had not worn it for two or three years – not since dressing up for local dances in Lee had come to an end when the wartime Blitz began. Even so, I did not think I looked too bad or the dress too dated and, snug in a fur coat borrowed from a friend of Mum's, I hurried happily along the Strand to the hotel.

Ann, who was one of those people who are always on time, was waiting to greet me and took me through to the ballroom area where, under the sparkling decorations hanging from the high ceilings, tables for different sized parties were closely packed around the dance floor. I was surprised to find that I was joining a party that included several older people. They turned out to be the host and hostess – parents of Ann's friends, Philippe and Stéphane – plus other friends or relatives. Ann had explained to me that the Lejeunes were an Anglo-Belgian family. It certainly added an exotic extra to the evening in my eyes, especially as the conversation at table proved to be in a mixture of English and French because, although all the Lejeunes were bilingual, some of their guests (including me) were not. It soon emerged that Philippe, the older of the brothers, was married; but his wife was not there, as she was expecting to go into labour at any moment with their first child. It dawned on me that it was because of this gap I had been invited.

The evening flew by, the noise and gaiety increasing steadily until it was hardly possible to hear anything but the hubbub itself. As the year moved to its end there was that febrile atmosphere of merriment, along with nostalgia and regret for the memories of past new years. When midnight struck, glasses were raised, the usual round of greetings began, and I found myself being embraced by Philippe. He was dark-eyed and good-looking, and solidly built as befitted his enthusiasm for rugby; his soft, silky moustache brushed my face as he kissed me with disturbing warmth.

I had intended to leave not long after midnight to catch the last train home, but the Lejeunes at first protested and then suggested that surely I should stay overnight at the hotel. When the parents made clear that this would of course be at their expense, I was persuaded. Someone went to book a room for me, and by the early hours of New Year's Day I was in bed and contentedly snuggling down to sleep. I was roused by a quiet knock on the door. Probably because I had drunk far more than I was used to, this did not alarm me. I assumed it must be some other reveller who had made a mistake about his or her room; but a second, slightly louder knock told me it was someone at my door and that I could not just lie there and hope whoever it was would go away. I got out of bed, grabbed the borrowed fur coat to cover myself, crossed the room and called out a bit nervously, 'Who is it?' 'It's me,' came the reply. 'Open the door!' Then, more urgently, 'Let me in! I'll explain.' I knew who it was, and fearful of disturbing whoever might be next door, I opened the door. Philippe pushed past me into the room.

His story was that he had somehow missed his parents, who were driving home to their house in a suburb in north-west London, and who were to have dropped him off at his flat on their way. He had tried unsuccessfully, he said, to get a taxi home. It didn't sound very convincing, but he was in the room and I did not feel I had much choice other than to agree that he could make himself comfortable in the armchair until morning.

I was soon asleep again, but not for long. Soon I was woken by Philippe slipping in beside me, complaining of being cold. Although I tried to be indignant, in fact I found it hard not to laugh. But when Philippe refused to move out of the bed I got out and went across to the armchair, this time using the borrowed fur coat as a blanket as well as to cover my nakedness. Thereafter a crazy game of in and out, and back and forth, went on until, at what must have been close to dawn, I gave in.

In the late 1940s, adultery (or, in my case, fornication) in a hotel room was not taken lightly, and when morning arrived I began to fear a shameful encounter with the management. I realized that for Philippe this could not have been the new experience it was for me when he assured me that there was nothing to worry about. He would go down first; I was to follow a exactly three minutes later. To my astonishment, when – with a thumping heart – I arrived at reception, I found him chatting amiably with the man behind the desk. As I walked in he looked across at me, gave a genial smile all round, and said, 'Are, there she is!'

'How did you manage it?' I asked him as, arm in arm and in buoyant mood, we walked along the Strand against the flow of people in sober dress on their way to work. (I had hitched up my long taffeta dress so that it did not show under the fur coat, and hoped it would not fall down.) Philippe explained: 'I just came down in the lift, walked out, came back in, and then asked at reception if you had left.'

I did not tell Ann what had happened, nor that I later met Philippe again. I was not in love with him, nor he with me. I knew, and he knew, that once his wife had the baby (which she did soon afterwards) our very brief but enjoyable affair must end. One reason that I could not tell Ann about what had happened was because I feared she would be shocked; and I knew that, being a friend of Philippe's wife, she would rightly also have been angry. It went without saying that Mum and Dad and my brothers would have been disgusted if they had known, just as Rose and her husband would have been. Even Pluckie, with whom I shared what we liked to think of as our liberated views, would I felt have been shocked. I seemed to be getting into a false position with almost everyone and surely, I thought, this sort of immoral behaviour was not right for a would-be social worker.

*

Such worries did not stop me setting off eagerly five days later to begin the next step in my burgeoning career. This was to be two months of 'practical experience' in one of the Family Welfare Association's offices. Set up in 1869 by philanthropic Victorians (and then called the Charity Organisation Society), the organization had played a historic role in the development of social work. A period working with FWA had long been considered an essential part of the training for social work students. My 'field-work placement', as it was called, was to take place in Deptford. I knew it slightly; it was only a mile or two away from Lee, and I had been there on shopping expeditions with Mum, who had probably heard about its cheap food markets from Grandad.

The Deptford branch of the Family Welfare Association had its offices above shops on the north side of the Broadway. The general office was on the first floor and had three large sash-windows looking out on to a busy crossroads. On the other side of the road were more shops, and rising behind them a grim-looking red-brick building called Carrington Lodge, a lodging-house run by the London County Council for homeless men.

On arriving at FWA, I was ushered into a smaller room leading off the general office to meet Miss Sanderson. She was tall and thin, probably in her forties, with fine light brown hair cut short, and wore a beige cardigan, brown skirt and low-heeled, lace-up shoes. Her detached and appraising look immediately conveyed to me that, as one in a long line of students under her supervision, I was already being assessed.

A brisk run-down on the organization of the office preceded a description of the neighbourhood. Next came an equally brief outline of what I would be doing, and then Miss Sanderson took me to a battered Edwardian desk in the outer office which, she told me, would be mine for the next eight weeks. I was introduced to the other occupants of the office. Miss Jenkins, a social worker, was a bespectacled, stockily built woman dressed all in brown. Her dark hair looked as if it needed a good comb-through, but she gave me a welcoming smile. A remarkably pretty young woman sitting at a desk next to mine proved to be a student 'on placement' from the London School of Economics who looked much too young for social work (and who confessed to me later that she knew this and so put on steel-rimmed glasses from Woolworth's when she went on home visits).

Settled at my desk I tried, not very successfully, to concentrate on the various papers and instruction booklets it was suggested I should read and digest – the view below of traffic and people was far more interesting. A few minutes later Miss Sanderson reappeared from her sanctum and put down another file on my desk. 'Miss Noble, these are the case-notes of one of our families,' she said. 'I want you to write a letter making an appointment to visit them.' A simple task, one might think. But I did not, and I took so long over it that, by the time I had finished, Miss Sanderson had gone off to a lunchtime meeting. I was rather glad she had, and left my attempt on her desk to await her return.

Pretty soon after she returned, she re-emerged from her room. To my alarm, as she crossed the room, I saw that she was holding my draft in front of her as if it had a dangerous substance on it or a nasty smell. 'Miss Noble,' she said in her brisk, no-nonsense manner. 'Do you *normally* use stuffy expressions like "With regard to your recent request, a home visit will be made on Tuesday, unless notified that this is not convenient"? No? Of course you don't! Well then, write this letter again in the way you would write to a friend you want to see.' It was a revelation to me that the stilted style I had assumed to be called for was not only unnecessary but – at least in Miss Sanderson's view – quite unacceptable, and that writing in everyday language was actually thought better.

Another surprising discovery I made in the days that followed was that, although only two miles away from Lee, Deptford was strangely foreign ground. I had no idea then that the Victorian housing reformer, Octavia Hill, had struggled – largely unsuccessfully – with the poverty and problems of the district more than half a century earlier. Nor that, at around the same time, my own grandfather had regularly taken on the drunks, local bullies and wife-beaters he met while treading the beat on these same streets as a young policeman.

If I had known about either, perhaps it would have been less of a shock when I was sent out on my first home visit to a poor Irish family living in one of the nearby slums. I arrived to find the front door open, and when I knocked a bedraggled woman appeared in the hall and directed me upstairs to the first-floor landing with instructions to knock again on the right-hand door. I found myself facing a threateningly sullen-looking man with the florid complexion of the heavy drinker. Without preamble he told me brusquely that his wife was out, but when I explained that I had come from the FWA's office he made an effort to curb his sullenness and invited me in. The Doyles were well known to the agency, and my job on this visit was to find out about their current problems and what could be done to help them.

The first thing I had noticed as I climbed the stairs was that many of the banisters were missing and that in this dilapidated terraced house there was not even worn lino to cover the treads. Even so, I was not prepared for what I saw when I followed Mr Doyle into the room which, for this family, proved to be all they could claim as a home. The real shock came as I cautiously looked round the room. 'To think such squalor can still exist!' I scribbled in my journal that night. 'Surely I can never forget that smoke-filled room, the mouldy cabbage in the corner, the bowl with the dirty water on the bare boards, the toddler wandering about in threadbare shirt and no shoes. Nor the horror I felt when Mr Doyle said in his heavy Irish accent, but so *casually*, "There's another behind you" – and I turned and saw a pile of rags on the bare springs of the bed, and hidden in the rags a dirty, tiny baby.' I have indeed never forgotten that visit, and I also remember still the relief with which I escaped from the house on that day. What I can't recall, or even imagine, is what good my visit could possibly have done.

I knew it was not for me to disparage the Doyles, since I had already learnt that the aim of social work was to try to understand, not to judge. Yet the plight of the children in that home did make this difficult. It was easy to see that poverty and ignorance explained a lot, but harder to exonerate the father from some blame. I don't believe I ever had such doubts over another unfortunate whom Miss Sanderson decided to put in my care, and I could not have foreseen the effect this next encounter was to have on my own life.

5

Mr White Protests

Mr White came shambling into the office, with his toes sticking out of the ends of his worn-out shoes, his clothes in rags and his grey hair almost as long and tangled as his beard. He was greeted like an old friend by Miss Jenkins, and almost as warmly by Miss Sanderson.

Mr White was an FWA regular. When he was not on the tramp elsewhere, he lived over the road at the common lodging-house. He would turn up at FWA hoping to get kitted up when his clothes wore out. He was used to the ways of the agency and took it for granted that before he got them he had to accept the conditions laid down, which were always the same: that he should first get a haircut and shave. Given the money to do this by Miss Sanderson, he was told to come back when the barbering was done, which he did a day or two later.

Again he was greeted warmly, and complimented on his short-back-and-sides haircut and clean-shaven chin, which had certainly improved his appearance. 'Now Miss Noble,' said Miss Sanderson, 'we must see what we can do to make Mr White even smarter. If you'll just wait a minute, Mr White, while Miss Noble puts on her coat, she can go with you straight away.' My heart sank as, having beckoned me into her office at the end of this announcement, Miss Sanderson handed over ten shillings and told me cheerfully that 'There are several second-hand clothes shops nearby – Mr White knows where they are. Get him a good pair of shoes, socks, trousers and a warm overcoat.'

It was a weird experience wandering in and out of second-hand shops with this queer, shambling fellow beside me. I was embarrassed for both of us, aware that we must have made an odd couple – one a neatly dressed, bloomingly young woman and this shabby tramp with his flapping shoes. It was difficult for me to make out what Mr White was saying as we walked along, side by side, because he not only mumbled but had a halting stutter. I could not help wondering how many students before me he had been forced to trail around with like this.

Following where Mr White led, I went with him to several shops before we found what was needed. To avoid further embarrassment for both of us I waited outside the shops, hovering by the doorway. I felt sure that I ought to have gone inside and taken charge, but I was beginning to warm to Mr White and I could not inflict this further indignity on him. At the end of our expedition he went off across the road to the 'doss-house' with his bundle of new clothes under his arm, while I returned to the office taking his new (or rather, second-hand) shoes with me, because Miss Sanderson's instructions were that he must bring in his ragged clothes before he could be given the new shoes.

As agreed, he came back the next morning and it was then that we had our first real talk. Mr White followed me into the small room set aside for seeing people in private, making a kind of low, growling noise as he did so. It was no more than a mild protest, for he knew the rules better than I did. I think it was at this moment that I began to get through to him, because in his way he tried to make clear that not only did he know the rules but, out of a strange sense of fairness, aimed to keep to them: 'Card for c-c-card,' he told me from the defensive position he had taken up on the other side of the mahogany table, 'I'll p-play your game.'

Under Miss Sanderson's instructions, my game had to include some questions about how he was getting on and what he had been doing. His answers on the state of his wheezing chest were more willingly given than those on where he had been to or come from, but gradually I wheedled more from him. He had grown up in an orphanage where he had been called out by number to be given his weekly supply of socks and linen, joined the Merchant Marine as soon as he could leave, and been at sea until he got 'too old for it'. He said he was sixty-four years old, although he seemed older, and his stumbling gait and vagueness about what he had done in the war suggested that his working days, whether on land or sea, had been over for a good many years.

By the end of our talk Mr White and I were getting on well – perhaps rather too well, I thought, when he came back three days running. It was exhausting work listening patiently to his mixture of complaints about the harsh house rules of Carrington Lodge, the rudeness of the local shop-keepers or my failure to get another 'loan' for him from the FWA petty cash. 'One visit from my tramp, Mr White, would have exhausted most students,' I grumbled in my journal, 'and I've had four! No doubt I am "green", but I feel desperately sorry for the man. Chiefly because I see no hope of really helping him – or of anyone else doing so. Yet obviously, despite his alternating moods of aggressiveness and mumbled good-humour, in a way the poor old fellow (Old? At sixty-four?) has not yet given up hope.'

It was the hope that I saw, or imagined I saw, in Mr White that made me eager to make a more positive contribution to his prospects; and after I visited Carrington Lodge, where the grim surroundings and the smell of despair seemed to belong to a distant past, I was even more concerned to do so. 'Surely there must be something better for down-and-outs than that sort of place!' I protested to Miss Jenkins when I got back. She said, not unsympathetically but firmly, that in her experience attempts to change the way of life of men who had lived rough for as long as Mr White had were almost invariably doomed to fail; but if I wanted to try, I might get in touch with one hostel she had heard of, where the aim was not only to give shelter but to 'rehabilitate' through jobs and resettlement.

The next time that Mr White appeared I told him about this place where there were people who really could help him. At the very least, I said (taking as gospel what I had heard from Miss Jenkins), he would find this hostel better than the awful Carrington Lodge. I wrote out the address on a scrap of paper, and passed on the instructions Miss Jenkins had given me on how he could get there. As I handed him the fare for the journey, Mr White shuffled about and looked doubtfully at the coins in his hand before shambling off, mumbling as he went that he 'm-might t-try it – or m-might not'.

Two days later Mr White came back, but this time he was not so much mumbling as spluttering with incoherent rage, and this time it was I who was glad to have the solid wood table like a barrier between us. 'Th-th-that place,' he puffed out, his poor chest heaving and wheezing alarmingly. '*You* sent me there! I w-w-wouldn't s-s-send a *dog* to that place.' Dismayed, I did my best to persuade him to tell me what had gone wrong, but he would say no more and left in the same angry mood.

After he had left I took the matter up with Miss Jenkins, but she was as puzzled as I was about what could have caused Mr White such distress. It was hard to imagine anything being worse than the dreadful Carrington Lodge, especially this new hostel which supposedly had such good intentions. 'Why don't you go and see for yourself what it's like?' suggested Miss Jenkins – a suggestion which, it occurred to me, might have been better put before I had sent Mr White along.

The voice at the end of the telephone when I rang the hostel was agreeably friendly. It made it easy to explain the reason for my call and why I wanted to come and see the hostel for myself. Known simply as 'the Hungerford', I was told by Miss Jenkins, it had been set up by the West London Mission, one of whose leading figures was the Revd Dr Donald Soper, Methodist minister at Kingsway Hall. (He was already so well known as a regular performer at Speakers' Corner in Hyde Park that even Mum and Dad knew of him by name.) Perhaps it was knowing all this that led me to think the person to whom I was talking at the Hungerford must himself be a member of the Methodist clergy. In my mind's eye, cued by the well-spoken, good-mannered tones, I saw a studious young man in cassock and dog-collar. 'We work on a rota here,' he said. 'Why not come when I am on evening duty, and I can show you around?' Was this apparent eagerness to be helpful further evidence of Christian goodwill? I wondered.

My eight weeks' placement at FWA was coming to an end. Mr White had not come back and, Miss Sanderson warned me, he had probably gone off in a huff for another few months. She kindly made clear that, in her eyes, I had done well enough with poor Mr White, but I had my doubts. Why should I have imagined that I had built a special relationship with him? Why should I have dared to suppose that I could really help with his problems, let alone understand his worries or his character? Was I cut out to be a social worker at all? Maybe not, but at least I ought, if I could – and having fixed an appointment with the voice – try to find out what had gone so awry for Mr White at the Hungerford, and even though it was unlikely I would ever see him again.

It happened that the hostel was off Kennington Road, in Wincott Street and very near to St Mary's Gardens where Pluckie was back living with her parents. When she heard about my proposed visit she invited me to tea. She had just finished a painting of St John, she said, and I would be the first to see it. In its moralistic style and rich colouring the picture owed much to her enthusiasm, which I had come to share, for El Greco. I envied her a talent that could be so expressive. Afterwards, we walked round to the hostel together, where she left me to find my way into what turned out to be a very unimposing building, more like an abandoned workshop than a hostel. I found out later that it was said to be the old casual ward of Lambeth's former Poor Law Institution.

The entrance was through a narrow, green wooden door in a high brick wall and led into a small courtyard where an unkempt little man – clearly a tramp – was hanging about. He directed me to 'the office' just inside the building and off a long, dark passageway. Looking in through the glass-panelled door, I saw a bespectacled young man with a pale complexion and a shock of light-brown hair above a large, high forehead. He was not in a dog-collar and looked too studious to be described as good-looking. 'Hallo!' he said, welcoming me in. 'I'm Peter Willmott.' It was the same pleasant voice I had heard on the telephone.

Looking around, I began to understand Mr White's reaction. Although in some ways better, the Hungerford looked

just as depressing, and in some ways it was worse than
Carrington Lodge. The fairly small common-room at the
Hungerford, despite its lavatory-looking tiled walls, did have
a peacefulness and more welcoming air about it than the
vast hall at Carrington Lodge, where numerous groups of
unkempt men crowded round the communal stoves with
battered saucepans and blackened frying-pans, creating a
hubbub, a smell of burnt fat and an atmosphere of Dicken-
sian pathos. At the Hungerford, staff did the cooking, such
as it was (there was only soup and rolls, and tea served in
'cups' made from empty condensed milk tins), and it was
served from a hatch in the kitchen. In both hostels the sleeping
quarters were bleak. There were scores, if not hundreds, of
cubicles on several floors at Carrington Lodge, each identi-
cal cubicle a model of barrack-like, hygienic coldness. At the
Hungerford, each cubicle had two bunks in it, one above
the other. With ten cubicles on either side of the long, dark
corridor, there were just two lavatories at the end for the
total of forty residents.

The better and worse points of the two hostels made a
good start to a mutually frank discussion, during which it
emerged that Peter Willmott was also a student, or at least
expecting to become one in the autumn. It was therefore
wonderful to discover that he was much concerned, as I believed
myself to be, about society and its problems, and about what
could or should be done about them in the post-war world
in which we now found ourselves. Furthermore, the opinions he expressed so confidently and eloquently suggested
that he assumed – wrongly but flatteringly – that I was as
well informed on all such subjects as he seemed to be. This
didn't stop me from asking innocently, 'Who is this Lewis
Mumford you keep referring to?' It brought the surprised
response: '*The Culture of Cities*? You haven't read it?' (I made
a mental note to try and fill this deplorable gap as soon as
I could.)

On the tram on my way homewards, I mulled over my
eventful evening. At first sight of him through the glass
panelling I knew that Peter Willmott had seemed less attractive in the flesh than that agreeable voice of his on the telephone had led me to hope. Yet within ten minutes I was

beguiled by his eloquence, in half an hour by his easy-going good humour and charm; and as I had left I caught myself thinking: I could be happy with this man. The very thought made me wonder at myself; for beneath the thought lay something unusually serious. It was as if I were looking ahead; almost as if I were weighing up the future. Ridiculous, really, I thought gloomily. I looked out of the tram window as we clanked along and swerved round the curving track past the shops in Lee High Road and got ready to get off at the next stop. It was ridiculous, because why should I ever see this man again? Well, I decided, I could at least scribble a note to thank him for the visit.

6
Baby-sitter

Having reached what seemed to me the advanced age of twenty-five, and almost convinced by this time that my future life and happiness must be found in the career in social work for which I was training, I did not regret the lost opportunities for marriage. Even though I had come to half believe that rare marriages – like the 'partnership' the Webbs were said to have enjoyed – could be different, I still feared that marriage in general was a sort of cul-de-sac of life. The trouble was that a future without marriage meant one sacrifice that I was not sure I wanted to meet.

It must have been mixed feelings like these that led one night to a telling dream which seemed to revolve around my friends, Pat and Frank, who had just had their second baby. In the dream, as I noted down in my ubiquitous journal: 'I met Pat, and she had baby Penelope, but seemed to be estranged from Frank. I asked her not to make it clear to anyone else that *my* baby was illegitimate. It was a bonny baby, but the complications about feeding it were obviously mixed up with seeing the Browns' baby in that terrible room in Deptford.'

I liked children, and enjoyed looking after Pat and Frank's son Nick, though I wouldn't have liked it all the time. So why had I dreamt of having a baby of my own? Was it, as I 'interpreted' it (and influenced by what I had learnt about Freud), because I wanted a baby, but 'without all the suburban trimmings of married life'? With a little more insight I might have seen that the 'terrible room' of the Doyles in my dream was not warning me off 'suburban trimmings' but the

*

stigma and impoverishment then likely to result from having an illegitimate baby.

I had got to know Pat before I left school. She was the sister of my first boy-friend, Ben Merriman, and we had met when he took me home to meet his welcoming family. With her very black hair and grey-green eyes, Pat had a white complexion and lips which, although thin, in repose were almost the shape of a flattened heart. She had an aquiline nose which was a little too long, and stubby hands with beautifully shaped nails. Her keen sense of the pretentious went with a barblike wit that could deflate the unwary. As painfully honest with herself as she was with others, she was also far kinder and more generous than most, or than her frequent verbal barbs sometimes suggested.

It was during the war that Ben had brought Frank, a fellow-officer in the wartime Royal Naval Reserve, to meet the invariably hospitable Merrimans at their home in Forest Hill. Slimly built, fine-boned and well spoken, Frank could have been the model of the 'typically British' naval officer of wartime propaganda films, although he was in fact Irish. He had spent a large part of the war on convoy patrol, which meant weaving devious and dangerous routes across the icy arctic waters of the North Atlantic under constant threat of attack by U-boats. Reserved, high principled and yet sometimes touchy, qualities which had no doubt been honed more by his naval experiences than his Irish origins, Frank was also a delightfully provocative conversationalist. As happened so often in the heightened atmosphere of wartime, Pat and Frank, having met and fallen in love, had grabbed at happiness and got married as soon as they could. Which is how one day, when I was on leave from the WAAF and had decided to pay a surprise visit to the Merrimans, I found I had arrived in the middle of the wedding reception.

About a year later little Nicholas was born, and by the time Pat was coping with her second baby, Penny (the subject of my dream), Frank had been demobilized and was busy establishing himself in a new career. With the stresses of post-war shortages added to those of adjusting to married life and its ties, it was not an easy time for either of them. But one way in which the young family had been lucky was in getting a flat during a period when, as a result of the war, the housing shortage was acute. They had got it only because Pat's aunt was able to speak to the landlord when she heard that the tenant in the flat next to her own was to move. Built around the turn of the century, the flat was a above a row of shops on a busy bus route in East Sheen. It was self-contained but a dark and gloomy place, with a cold north-facing drawing-room at the front, two bedrooms, and a kitchen at the back with a scullery off it which was the only really sunny spot.

Like most young parents, Pat and Frank found being cata-pulted into parenting hard going. With social life inevitably cut back, friends' visits were important and I was always welcome. Sometimes I went for a meal, sometimes to stay for a weekend, and occasionally to baby-sit so that they could have an evening out together. Although Pat had never had ambitions to be more than a good wife and mother, she had no patience with romantic illusions about the 'joys of mother-hood' and loved getting away from bottles and nappies and the wearisome trivialities of child-rearing whenever she could – and that wasn't very often.

Pat breezily admitted that she could make no great claims to understand or love children in general, and also that she knew that even with little Nick, adorable as he was, she was often cross and impatient. She drily pointed out too that it was easy for me to claim to love children – and to be far more patient with her son than she was – because I did not have to look after him day after day, as well as doing house-work, shopping and everything else that she, as a housewife, had to do. It was true that I believed I was 'good with children' (and that with unconscionable smugness I did credit myself with having more understanding of them than Pat); but I had no such illusion about babies and did not feel at all confident when I agreed to look after the new baby and Nick for an evening so that Pat and Frank could go out.

Pat's eagerness to get away, which was reflected in her apparent lack of concern about leaving the baby with me, left me feeling even more uneasy. 'There are plenty of clean nappies,' she said hurriedly, at the same time looking all over the place to find a mislaid handbag, 'and her bottle's ready.

Just put it in a basin of hot water for a minute or two for her ten o'clock feed. And if she wakes earlier – and she does sometimes – just change her nappy and give her a spoonful of gripe-water and she'll probably go off again.' Then, clearly delighted at the thought of their evening out, she and Frank urged Nick to 'be a good boy', gave him a hug and a kiss, and were off.

To my dismay, even before Nick was asleep the baby had begun to yell. It was only seven-thirty, much too early to give her the bottle. Nervously I picked her up, carried her to the kitchen and, following Pat's instructions with some difficulty, changed her terry towelling nappy and then tried out the gripe-water. It was useless, as was pacing up and down, rocking, crooning, rechecking the nappy and its safety-pins, and – as desperation increased – asking Nick 'What does Mummy do?'

When the screams brought Pat's aunt running in from next door to find out what was wrong, it seemed for a moment that relief had come. But alas, Aunt Cis, who had never had children, proved no more successful with soothing the frantic baby than I was. We were soon both equally near to a state of panic; both equally afraid how this tiny, bawling, red-faced 'thing' could hope to survive much longer the paroxysms of rage by which it seemed to be consumed. Perhaps, Aunt Cis suggested tentatively, with all the energy the baby had used up in this dreadful screaming, she was already hungry, even though it was far too early for her feed.

With relief, I agreed, and we got out the bottle. It was what I had been wanting to do for what seemed like for ever; but, alas, this too proved no solution. Although baby Penny attacked the bottle with amazing energy, considering how much she had used up already, the harder she sucked, the more frustrated she became. Scarlet-faced, she now alternated frenzied sucking with screams. It dawned on us that we were confronting a new horror: virtually no milk was getting through the teat. 'We'll have to make the hole larger. Where does Pat keep her sewing things?' I asked. Aunt Cis didn't know, so she scuttled back to her flat to find a needle. It was no good. Hard as we tried – first to enlarge the hole with the needle, then with growing despair to puncture new

ones by jabbing with scissors – still the poor babe could get
no milk through. As a last resort we tried to spoon the milk
in but by this time Penny, who in her own way was no doubt
as despairing as we were, was not willing to stop crying long
enough to co-operate. She seemed unnervingly more inclined
to choke on the milk being trickled in to her than to swallow
it.

Interminable though the evening had become, time was
passing, and at last the welcome noise of a key in the door
announced Pat and Frank were back. Disappointed though
she must have been at what they had returned to, Pat said
with her usual laconic humour, 'Oh Lor! You've had a good
evening, I see.' When she realized what had happened, she
said to Frank, 'Where's your lighter?' And to us, 'It's just
that you must heat the needle to make the hole bigger.' It
worked like magic.

Very soon after, while Penny at last slept and Aunt Cis
crept away with relief to her own bed next door, Pat, Frank
and I settled down in the kitchen for a nightcap that lasted
far too long. When Penny's cries roused us all again three or
four hours later, I heard Pat padding along the passageway.
I knew that she would be warming up another bottle in a
kitchen where the stove would no longer be giving out any
warmth. Maybe I felt a slight twinge of guilt as I snuggled
down in my warm bed and pulled up the blankets to deaden
the sound of the baby's cries; but it was not strong enough
to stop me from slipping back into deep, dreamless sleep.

7

Bliss

Two or three weeks after my visit to the Hungerford I met my new friend again. This time it was under the clock at Charing Cross Station. I'd come up on the train from Lee, where I was enjoying a fortnight's 'study break' before the return to Bloomsbury for another eight weeks of lectures and 'visits of observation'. Peter Willmott had just come back from a week's visit to his father and stepmother who lived in the country.

By this time I knew that even before he had received my thank-you letter he had telephoned FWA to invite me out. Finding that I was no longer there he asked for my address. He was told that this could not be given to him, although if he wrote care of the agency the letter would be forwarded. I explained that this was because of Miss Sanderson's high standards about confidentiality. Peter declared it was fussiness. In any case, before he had time to contact me through this roundabout route, my letter had reached him. We met at Charing Cross a few days later.

Peter suggested that we might lunch at the Vega, a restaurant I had heard of but never been to. It was in Leicester Square, and at the time unique because vegetarianism was far less common then and indeed considered to be cranky. That Peter proclaimed *he* was a vegetarian was one of the oddities that made him seem out of the ordinary. Although I did not much like the food at the restaurant, this hardly mattered, since the occasion had so much spice of its own. After lunch, we took a long walk through the parks made specially beautiful by the early signs of spring. Through the long afternoon we talked about ourselves – our families, our past lives, but above all our ambitions for the future.

After one of our lectures on social psychology (given by Dr Wilson, the impressively wise, humane – and rather sad – psychiatrist from the Tavistock Institute), I told Ann about my new friend. As we sat munching sandwiches under the plane trees in the square I gaily reported: 'He's got a terrific sense of humour, but he's quite a curiosity.' Ann asked, 'What on earth do you mean?' I tried to explain. 'Well, he's not only a vegetarian, but says he was an anarchist. And what's more, he loathes his parents. It sounds like a pretty unhealthy combination, doesn't it?'

This was hardly the dispassionate appraisal that I pretended to be making. For, unhealthy though the signs might have been, by the time I spoke to Ann hardly a day went by when I did not see Peter. As blossom bloomed, he was introducing me to more of a London excitingly different from the one I had known until then. We went to dinner at the riverside Prospect of Whitby in Wapping. Born and reared in south London as I had been, north of the river was to me a foreign land. I listened absorbed to Peter's views on the character of east London and its people, and at the same time savoured the surroundings.

Through the bay window I could see the muddy waters of the Thames lapping against old timbered pylons. Across the dark, low-ceilinged room brightened by the table-cloths of red and white check I could look surreptitiously at Peter King, a well-known broadcaster whom, in some mysterious way in that pre-television age, Peter had recognized. As curious to know about my world as I was about his, on another evening Peter came to south London. This time the walk through Greenwich Park and across Blackheath to the Crown, one of the pubs in the village, was an introduction for Peter to the familiar places I had known since childhood. It was a damp evening, and with everything sparkling in bright fresh green it had never looked so lovely.

There were times, inevitably, when things went less well, like the Sunday morning we met to attend a mass, of all things, considering what sturdy agnostics we both proclaimed ourselves to be, at Brompton Oratory. It was another of Peter's suggestions. Religion was part of the culture of our society, Peter explained, and therefore something in which we should take an objective interest. On top of this, he claimed, the Roman Catholic liturgy was itself an aesthetic experience by which anyone of sensibility could not fail to be touched.

Unfortunately, as it must have seemed to Peter, my lack of sensibility was exposed when I turned up for the occasion wearing green slacks. I was faced by a disapproving look, at which my first puzzled reaction turned to indignation when Peter solemnly explained that my slacks were, in his view, 'an error of judgement'. It was because Peter seemed to have such admirable opinions on practically anything, could express what he thought with such enviable confidence, and usually seemed so unconcerned about conventions, that my fury was so aroused at this unexpected decree. We parted that day on cool terms, but the magnetic spell between us quickly drew us together again. Being apart was too painful.

Peter, who had been living away from his parents since the age of sixteen, turned out to have had a very different upbringing from my own. Whereas my earliest memory was of holding my brother's hand on the day my mother and father came home from the nursing home with the new baby, Peter's was of his mother, Dorothy, saying, as he stood at her bedside, 'Poor Peter, what will become of him?' Sadly, it was not only his earliest memory, but almost the last, for Dorothy died before he was four years old. For a while he was left in the care of a daily housekeeper, but after village gossip reached Benjamin Willmott that his son was being ill-treated, he offered a home to his wife's sister, Grace. Trapped in an unhappy marriage from which she wanted to escape, Grace moved in, bringing her two young daughters with her.

In time, aunt became stepmother, but the relationship with her dead sister's child remained an uneasy one. When the war began, Peter was evacuated to the country with his school, and afterwards he never returned to live for more than a week or two with his father and stepmother. It was no doubt because of this early launch into independence that – although not without 'errors of judgement' of his own – Peter had a maturity which I still lacked.

When Peter, to his parents' disappointment, dropped out of school at sixteen, his father had him apprenticed as a motor mechanic, hoping that this might keep his only son safe, in a reserved occupation for the duration of the war. Found lodgings in Luton with a working-class family in which there was a boy of his own age, Peter saw with amazement – and some envy – what an indulgent maternal affection could mean. Later, as the war years ground on, he was called up, not into the forces, but as a 'Bevin boy' to work in the mines. He was sent to the Rhondda in South Wales to work as a miner's 'butty' where he lived in a hostel with other Bevin boys. The Welsh culture and the courage and character of the miners were to leave an indelible impression upon him, but the long hours of shovelling in underground seams too narrow to stand up in was hot, hard work, for which he was ill-equipped. Work as an apprentice in the factory had been hard and tedious, but as nothing compared with that in the mines.

As a result of an attack of measles when Peter was only eighteen months old, his eyesight was poor, and from that early age he had had to wear spectacles. Down the mine this proved a serious handicap. Because of the mixture of coal-dust and sweat that coated his glasses, much of the time his vision was restricted to what he could see through the narrow channels cleared by sweat as it trickled down his lenses.

On 14 August 1945, when Japan surrendered and the war had at last ended, Peter was called for a medical review. He was found to have developed the miner's disease, nystagmus, and declared unfit for further work in the mines although fit for military service. On the same day Peter discovered (by a surreptious look at his papers) that he was regarded as 'officer material', but as he had by this time decided that he was a pacifist he refused to join the forces. He felt that he was now more in sympathy with the Quakers' campaign for 'reconciliation' and the Friends Relief Service, which was already at work sending clothes and teams of relief workers into Germany and the former occupied countries of Europe.

Peter started work for the Friends Relief Service by packing bales of clothing to ship to Europe in one of the warehouses. He was promoted soon after to become assistant quartermaster managing stores and provisions for all the hostels of the Friends Relief Service and the Friends Ambulance Units in London, and then promoted again to work in the publicity department of the head office at Euston. So it was, through the encouragement of the Quakers (who had noticed his aptitude for writing), that he found himself for the first time doing work of a kind he could wholly enjoy. In late 1946 he volunteered to go off on a fund-raising tour. In that particularly bitter winter he drove the Friends Relief Service van across East Anglia and the Home Counties, stopping at a different place each night to present a publicity film on the relief work in Europe.

By the spring of 1947 the time had come for Peter to think about a more permanent future career, and it was while he was doing so that he heard through his Quaker connections of the post at the Hungerford. One of the advantages of the work with the Friends had been that hostel accommodation went with the job, and he was glad to find that the Hungerford also could offer him a place to live. This time it was in a flat on the floor above the hostel which had in earlier times been for the use of the master of the casual ward. The flat had two living-rooms, a lavatory and primitive bathroom, but no kitchen. A dark stairway off the entrance to the hostel led up to the rooms and gave them a mews-like atmosphere.

Peter had taken over one room as a bed-sitter. It was a spacious room at the front of the building. There were two large sash-windows, under one of which was Peter's metal-framed single bed, while under the other stood a plain wood table on which were placed two gas rings, one or two plates, cups and a few bits of cutlery. The bare floor-boards Peter had stained black, and there was one rug – colourless and worn – in front of an ancient gas fire that made popping and sputtering noises when lit. Invited for supper, I was given on my first visit a tin of macedoines, warmed up on one of the gas rings, mixed with a few dried dates and served up on a tin plate with a glass of beer. Followed by bread and cheese, then some chocolate with coffee, this second experience of a vegetarian meal seemed to me admirably carefree and Bohemian. We ate sitting on the rug in front of the gas fire, and perfected the evening by making love in the single bed between Peter's shockingly grey sheets which (he later admitted) had not been changed for months.

The room overlooked the yard of the hostel I had so recently

crossed for the first time. Beyond the high brick wall was a
typical Lambeth street of small terraced houses. The room
faced south-west and was bright and very light, partly because there were no curtains at the windows. This also meant
that our *affaire* was not quite as private as I, at least, had
hoped. One day, just as I was climbing into bed with Peter,
I looked through the uncurtained window and saw a woman
staring in at us from her window across the way. It was disconcerting, even though I was not sure whether her expression was that of puzzled curiosity or shocked disgust!

Such prudish anxieties did not seem to bother Peter, whose
response to mine was to pin up one of his blankets across
the window when I visited him. I was less confident than he
was that this solved the problem. 'Supposing the neighbours
in the street complain?' I asked. 'Oh, but they won't,' said
Peter, who had got to know some of the local people. 'They
believe in being neighbourly, but in "keeping themselves to
themselves". They know it's not their concern what we do
in here.'

Unhappily, it soon became clear that my visits were not
only noticed but looked on with disapproval by some of Peter's
fellow-workers, who held to the more conventional view that
having sex – which they rightly deduced was taking place –
was immoral between an unmarried couple. One young but
priggish colleague (who was engaged to be married himself)
complained to Peter that he was bringing the hostel into
disrepute. I began to worry that famous Dr Donald Soper
might hear about us, but again Peter refused to be concerned.

I was spending so much time with this man that Mum
and Dad began to get more and more curious. 'He sounds
nice enough,' said Mum, dubiously, having spoken to Peter
on the telephone more than once. 'When are we going to
meet the latest?' teased Dad and my brothers. I knew that
they were all wondering if I might be at last getting ready to
settle down, which was no doubt the impression I was giving myself. I knew that I was reassessing my own views on
marriage, and indeed wondering what marriage to Peter would
be like. He had told me that, on the evening of our first
meeting, he had said to one of his colleagues after I left, 'I

have met the girl I want to marry.' Remembering my own first impression, it struck me that this seemed remarkably like 'love at first sight' – even though it didn't feel quite as I had imagined it would.

Increasingly involved though I was with Peter, I was not keen to take him home to meet my family. Although I no longer had the feeling of superiority towards Mum and Dad that had made my life – and theirs – miserable when I was a snobbish schoolgirl at the grammar school, I could still feel uneasy about my humble background. I was afraid Peter would find my family very unintellectual, and that they would find him beyond their ken. But when Peter began to show as much curiosity to meet them as they did to meet him, I knew that the day could no longer be delayed.

When he came down on the train, and I met him at Hither Green Station, I was determined to make the best of things, however they turned out. It was Easter Sunday, and I knew that Dad and 'the boys' would, as usual, come home from the pub in cheerful and cocky good humour, Dad probably pickled and smelling of beer and cigarette-smoke. I knew that conversation would not be at all on the sort of subjects that Peter and I found so absorbing. I knew that I would have to help Mum by taking into the living-room, one by one, the piled plates of the Sunday roast dinner that she, red-faced and sweaty, would serve out as fast as she could in the kitchen, shouting out as I carried the first plate through, 'Start! Don't let it get cold!'

Apprehensive though I was, I had to let Peter make of it what he could. The pleasant surprise was that he did not seem to find the situation difficult. When I began to trot backwards and forwards from the kitchen, he (sharing my views on equality between the sexes) jumped up and said politely, 'Let me help.' 'No, no. Sit down Pete,' said brother Wal in his loud, genial tone. No one I knew called Peter 'Pete', but my cousin Pete (who was always called Pete) added in his quieter, amiable way, 'Yes, sit down. You'll only be in the way out there.' Dad had his quizzical look on his face. I knew he was thinking, What sort of a fella is this she's brought home, now? I smiled brightly at Peter as he sat down again at the table. It wasn't too hard because I didn't want him to look around in the dark old kitchen, with its chipped sink and Mum's washing-line draped with underwear and tea-towels hanging over him.

On our way back to the station I realized how foolish my worrying had been when Peter said, 'I really like the way you are with your family. And they are obviously so fond of you.' Far from being contemptuous, as I had feared he might be, he seemed to appreciate my family more than I did. It was Mum's reaction that was disturbing, as I found out from cousin Ken later that evening. After Peter and I had left, this mother who, in the past, had revealed sometimes almost clairvoyant powers, firmly announced: 'Well, she won't marry *him*, that's sure.'

8

In at the Deep End

One day near the end of May I went back again to St Thomas's Hospital. I climbed the steps and went in under the columned portico feeling a little nervous but very happy at the prospect of spending the next eight weeks, not only again in this historic hospital but now as a student almoner. Casualty Sister, whose frilled and bestringed cap seemed even more gleaming white in the shade of the portico, was standing regally at the top of the steps, waiting and ready, as always, to make an instant decision on where to direct new arrivals.

Behind her was the vast open space where both casualty patients and out-patients waited (and known within St Thomas's as 'the Sorting Room'). Skirting round Sister, I crossed the hall and made my way to Miss Read's office on the other side of the the wide arcade that served as the hospital's main artery. Miss Read seemed almost as pleased to have me back again as I was to be there. She told me about the long history of hospital social work at St Thomas's. It was one of the first hospitals to employ 'lady almoners', and she now had over twenty on her staff. She explained that, despite her efforts to change over to the more up-to-date title of 'hospital social worker', most hospital staff and patients still stuck to the old name.

Could I work under pressure? she asked, because she was going to put me with Mrs Osman, the lady almoner in Casualty, where the work was not only very demanding but where one had to work very quickly. I probably sounded more confident than I felt when I replied lightly that I was sure I would be able to cope. 'That's good,' said Miss Read crisply. 'Now I'll take you along to Mrs Osman.'

We walked the few yards from Miss Read's office back to

Casualty. We stood for a moment in the centre of the huge, high-ceilinged hall, which also served as the crossing-point between the main entrance and the flagstoned way leading to the wards, as Miss Read pointed out the various treatment-rooms and offices around the hall. At both ends of the room many patients waiting to be seen were seated on the heavy, dark, wooden benches set out in lines like church pews. We made our way to one of the doors opening off the hall. This one was marked *Casualty Almoner*. The door was ajar and we could see that Mrs Osman was with a patient. We hovered outside until the patient came out, at which point Miss Read ushered me in and 'handed me over', as she put it, adding briskly as she left: 'I leave you in good hands.'

Mrs Osman, a beautiful young woman with golden-blonde hair, a peachy, slightly downy complexion and a gently determined look about her, was friendly in manner, but pointed out that she had so many more patients to see she could spend only a moment or two with me now. What she would like me to do was to sit at the desk facing her and wait until she could find a moment to explain things. Before the morning was over, and with the help of a form to guide me on the basic details I had to find out and note down, I was seeing my first patient.

Although at first I felt hot with fear, and my hands grew sticky with sweat, I soon realized that the people facing me were far more nervous than I was, and so I quickly forgot my own fears in the desire to ease theirs. Basically, Mrs Osman had explained, seeing the patients had two main purposes. One was to find out whether they had any worries with which we could help, and the other was to ask each patient at the end of the interview if he or she could make a donation to hospital funds. It was at this point I had to pick up and shake the small tin box that stood on my desk, explaining as I did so that the hospital depended on voluntary contributions. I seldom managed this part of the interview without embarrassment on my side, and too often on that of the patients, whose worn clothes and worried faces showed clearly enough how little they could afford.

In the weeks that followed, morning after morning passed by for me in a whirl of people and their problems. The afternoons were always quieter, and gave me an opportunity to discuss with Mrs Osman what could be done to help with the practical or financial problems that illness or accident had brought. I did not spend all the time at my desk. Sometimes I was given the job of taking a nervous or distressed patient to another part of the hospital. At other times, Mrs Osman sent me off on a home visit.

In that unquiet room where we could hear the constant din of trams grinding in their tracks along Lambeth Palace Road I must have seen dozens of patients; but out of the blur of men in caps and mufflers, and women in shabby brown coats and variable hats, only two or three stand out in my memory. There was the distraught young woman with wispy fair hair, clutching to her breast her 'baby' – a wide-eyed, pale-faced but chubby child of some ten or twelve months – who was enveloped in a white woollen shawl and, unlike the mother, quiet and docile. I watched, impressed and fascinated, as Mrs Osman spoke quietly and gently to the agitated woman and reassured her that no one was trying to poison her baby or wanted to take her away.

Mrs Osman gave me the job of escorting the poor woman to the psychiatric clinic to which she had been referred. It took some time and needed repeated reassurances from me to get her to the clinic, which was some way away, buried in the subterranean gloom of the basement. During our slow progress there I realized that, disturbed as she was, this poor woman had picked up our concern for her and her child – a concern that had blotted out my first instinctive fear of her madness.

Most days it was not a matter of blotting out fear but of facing the added sadness and hardship that the breakdown of health could bring to people who had always had to struggle to survive even in relatively favourable circumstances. Such was the man I was sent out one day to call on at home. He was in need of urgent treatment for cancer, Mrs Osman explained, but he had failed to come in as arranged. I was to make a home visit to find out why he had not come, and to try to persuade him of the importance of not delaying. I knew as soon as I walked into the little corner shop in one of the back streets of Lambeth that, behind the counter, was the patient I had come to see. Thin and pallid, he looked a very sad and sick man, but his face lit up when I explained who I was and why I had come. I can no longer remember the reason he gave why he had failed to keep the previous appointment, but it was clear that whatever it was he had regretted it. A week later, he stopped me in Casualty to greet me and shake my hand with a disproportionate warmth and gratitude. He was on his way to one of the wards. I wished him a rapid recovery with a confidence that, alas, I did not feel.

There was a great sense of excitement everywhere within the hospital by the time my last week came round. It was the beginning of July 1948, and the National Health Service was about to start. On the final days before the 'Appointed Day' in Casualty we joyfully abandoned the little tin boxes. It was the symbolic new beginning of a health service that was intended to be free to all.

Although I had survived well, as I thought, the pressure of working in Casualty at St Thomas's, I was more affected by it than I had realized. In fact, when I arrived at Hammersmith Hospital for my second stint of student practice, it felt as if I had not simply lost my nerve but suffered an attack more like shell-shock. When I found myself in the office of Hammersmith's Head Almoner and sat facing her across her desk I suspect she knew this at first glance.

A big-boned, exceptionally tall and very plain woman with large front teeth, Miss Enid Warren seemed at first sight an unlikely person to restore my desperate loss of confidence. But her calm manner, and the direct and steady look from her grey eyes were reassuring. Within minutes I was over-come with such relief that my eyes filled with tears. I hastily blinked them back – observed, I've no doubt, in the pause that followed, by the appraising grey eyes. 'Now Miss Noble,' said Miss Warren, slowly and carefully, 'how would you like to start off? Some students like nothing better than to be thrown straight into the fray. Others prefer to take their time, to sit in the corner for a few days, and absorb things by just listening and watching.'

Gratefully lurking at my desk during those first few days, I had time to compare the ancient voluntary hospital I had just left with the one in which I now found myself. Although it had built up a prestige of its own as the only centre in Britain at the time for postgraduate medical studies, Hammersmith Hospital lacked the voluntary traditions and prestige of St Thomas's. Until the National Health Service took over, Hammersmith Hospital had been under the management of the London County Council, which had not yet entirely abolished its links with the Poor Law. Looking for signs of these different origins I decided that the 'lady almoners' of St Thomas's had a gentle charm and grace – and perhaps also a slight condescension – that was quite different from the courteous, kindly but cooler professional attitude of the 'hospital almoner' at Hammersmith. I also decided that the utilitarian uniforms of the nurses at Hammersmith, although less romantic than the frills and bows of the 'Nightingale' nurses of St Thomas's, were perhaps more in tune with our age; and so were the more modern Hammersmith buildings and furnishings, even though these seemed to lack the high polish and solidity of those at St Thomas's.

Restored by the chance to unwind through such musing, I was soon again ready for the fray. This time the desk at which I sat was one of the three in Miss Warren's own office. Her desk faced the window; Miss Oswald, her deputy (whose supercilious manner, Oxford degree and membership of the Fabian Society were slightly awesome), had hers under the window; while mine was in an inconspicuous place almost behind the door. Miss Warren took her responsibilities for students seriously. Each week, she explained, she would be discussing with me the patients I saw, but I could raise any problems I had with her as and when they came up. This was not quite so easy as it sounded, because she was out of the office as often as in it, either seeing patients herself on one of the wards, lecturing nursing and medical staff about the personal problems ill-health and disablement could bring, or out at committees and other meetings promoting the cause of professional social work to which she was utterly dedicated.

Miss Warren involved herself in these many activities without any outward signs of pressure. She never seemed impatient or in a hurry; she was never devious and, although she could be disconcertingly blunt, she had that rare talent of seeming to give her undivided attention to whomever she was talking. Invariably, she spoke in a firm yet fluting tone of voice; and whether she was speaking to the most exalted consultant, the most deferential patient or the humblest of students, each one was given the impression that she had all the time in the world for them.

Miss Warren was not without her little eccentricities, as I experienced one day when we discussed a young man I had seen on the ward who was about to be discharged. He was twenty-one years old and lived 'in digs'. The medics had referred him to us because he was thought to be at risk of developing tuberculosis. In our discussion on what might be done to help this young man, Miss Warren asked me about his eating habits. I had to admit it was not something I had thought about. 'Well now, he lives alone, and he probably does not eat well,' she said. 'Now it's very easy to grill tomatoes, and tomatoes on toast make a very nutritious breakfast. That's what he needs, and we must tell him' – by which she meant that I must do so. It led to an embarrassing few minutes beside the young man's bedside as I dutifully carried out Miss Warren's instructions, with little conviction on my part, and I fear even less on the young man's. Only years later did I discover that tomatoes held some magic quality for Miss Warren – so much so that she found it hard to believe that people could actually prefer wine or champagne to the tomato juice she regarded as the king of all tipples.

It was fortunate that I had so fully absorbed the lesson in literary style that Miss Sanderson had taught me at FWA, since at Hammersmith long and detailed reports were expected from students on their 'casework' with patients. One sunny afternoon I was sent off on a home visit for Dr Maxwell Fry, a consultant at the hospital who was doing exciting pioneering work with patients suffering from mental illness. Having first made clear that, in her view, being asked by so eminent a man to do such a visit was a privilege, Miss Warren carefully prepared me for it. This patient, she explained, complained of being depressed and the purpose of my visit was to form the best impression I could of the patient's home background so as to help Dr Fry in his diagnosis and decisions on treatment.

I set out through the unknown streets of amorphous west London and found my way to a small house not far from Wormwood Scrubs Prison. I couldn't help thinking as I walked past those fortified walls that having to live so close to such a grim building would probably be enough on its own to send me into permanent depression. Arrived at the patient's home, I quickly dismissed such an irrelevant thought and got down to concentrating, as I had been told to, on the 'home situation' on which I was to focus. After much re-writing, I ended up with a report that went something like this:

My visit to the Browns was made at 2.30 p.m. Mrs Brown came to the door, carrying her freshly dressed and fed two-month-old baby. Mrs Brown is a short, rather plump, natural-looking woman, with a quiet controlled manner. Mr Brown was at work.

The family have rooms on the first floor of the house.

There is no garden and no bathroom. Mrs Brown said that her husband had done all the painting and papering as the landlord does nothing. However, Mr Brown had decided he won't do anything else in the flat, and can't bear to be in it.

Mrs Brown says that she is worried at her husband's loss of weight, lack of appetite and inability to sleep. At work, he tells her, he is quite happy, but he can feel depression creeping over him on his way home. She says that they have always got on together and in fact in their thirteen years of married life have 'never had a cross word'. She does not argue with him, or snap at him, as she is the sort of person who can't bear to row. Her mother-in-law considers that she has pandered to him too much.

The first baby of this couple, who was born at the flat, died of meningitis. The baby had been left outside the front door and the pram was overturned by a child. Since the birth of her other babies, Mrs Brown has

always put them out on the landing in their pram when
they are indoors.

By the time Mr Brown went into the Army the
Browns had two children, one aged two years and the
other a baby. They were evacuated with Mrs Brown, and
when her husband returned home after the war the
children were five and three. They have a toy cupboard,
but because of the tenants on the ground floor below
they are allowed to play with them only on the table,
and are corrected if they drop things on the floor.

During the winter one child had mumps and another
pneumonia twice, and Mrs Brown puts this down to the
fact that she spends as much time as possible outdoors,
and dreads the winter because of this. (She says she still
has a doctor's bill of £5 outstanding.)

I asked Mrs Brown what she considered to be the
cause of her husband's illness. She said in decisive tones
that she was certain it was living in the flat. The family
have advertised for somewhere better to live and have
been on the housing list for almost two years.

For thousands of young families like the Browns the war
and its aftermath had brought marital or housing problems,
and sometimes both. It was a common plight that, before
long, I was to face painfully myself. I thought then, as I do
still, that Mrs Brown's own diagnosis that 'the flat was the
only problem' was not the whole story. On the other hand,
it did not need much insight or social work skill to guess
that a new home might have rapidly eased, if not cured, Mr
Brown's depression.

9

Under a Thatched Roof

By the time I left St Thomas's Hospital, even though 'still trying to find my way out of the whirl', I had discovered that 'amazingly, I can go on a whole day without an awareness of myself'. It was amazing because, outside work, all my time and thoughts continued to be absorbed by Peter, whose future plans were by then settled. He had been offered a place to study economics and politics at Ruskin College, Oxford, starting in October. The diploma course he was to take would last two years, but if as he hoped he was able to transfer to a degree course, his studies would go on for three or four years.

Neither he nor I had any doubts that this was the path he ought to follow, but it meant that just as I would be finishing my brief career as a student, he would start to be one. Sitting on a bench together in Embankment Gardens on a dulcet evening in early June I was dismayed to discover that, hard though we found it to be apart for even one day, Peter was assuming we might soon have to be separated for whole terms at a time. 'I hope you'll marry me when I've finished at Oxford,' he said. 'I don't think that's likely!' was my fierce response. 'I couldn't possibly just wait around for three years! Sorry, but I know how it will be. If you are in Oxford, and I am in London – or wherever it is I can get a job – I'll soon be gallivanting about with someone else, as I'm sure you will too.' It was another evening in which we parted coldly; but the powerful magnet of attraction between us was too strong to resist. A few days later we were back again in the Embankment Gardens, this time close by the statue of Gordon of Khartoum.

My protest (or was it an ultimatum?) had made Peter think

again. If I was not happy about waiting, why should we not get married now? he proposed. I could look for a job after I qualified at the big Radcliffe Hospital in Oxford, he suggested, and we could find digs there and so not be separated at all. Faced with Peter's new proposal, I was pitched into unexpected confusion. It was a mixed feeling of great happiness and gloomy apprehension as all the old thoughts of being caught in the trap of marriage – that point where life ended – reared up before me again with frightening force. Unable to sort out what I really felt, I responded with what I intended to be taken as light-hearted caution. 'I suppose if it doesn't work out we can always get a divorce,' I said. There was nothing light-hearted about Peter's reply, and again it took me aback. 'That is no way to go into marriage,' he said. I knew then that this man, this love, this time were in earnest.

A few days later Peter arranged that we should go down for the weekend to his parents' home in Great Chesterford, a village in a quite hilly, rural part of Essex, near Saffron Walden. We were not 'engaged' – being against such formalities on principle (though I am no clearer now than I was then what exactly this meant) – but as Peter had not in the past taken his women friends home, his family must have been as curious about me as I was about them. What would they be like, his father and stepmother, these 'horrible Conservatives' whom Peter told me soon after we met that he 'loathed'? (It later emerged that it was his stepmother he did not love, and that his main grievance against his father was that he had married – and seemed to love – this woman.)

Peter's father, Benjamin Willmott, was waiting at the station to meet us and drive us to the village in his comfortable, silver-grey Hillman Minx. Compared with the menfolk in my own family, he was not tall and he was also, I realized in the first few minutes, jollier, better spoken and far more gentlemanly than any of them were. Although it was the weekend, he was dressed in a sober suit, with striped shirt and tie and highly polished black shoes. When he raised his hat to greet me, I saw that he had a rather small head with precious little hair left on top. He also had a bushy, well-trimmed grey moustache that seemed to underline his baldness and his warmly pinkish face. In the short while we were in the car on the way to the cottage it became clear that Benjamin was an ebullient, garrulous and kindly extrovert – and also a snob who delighted in describing as we went through the village the class of its inhabitants. 'Lady Dorothy Neville lives there,' he said. 'She is related to the owner of Audley End. And there's George, he's a retired gardener and sometimes helps us now in the garden. He's a nice old boy, but he is under the misapprehension that "lilac" is pronounced "lilock", and nothing will shake him on that.' At this early stage in our acquaintance it seemed unwise for me to say that as 'lilock' was the word my Norfolk-born grandfather had always used, I was under the same misapprehension.

We turned right off the main street into a narrow lane and, to my delight, pulled up outside a low, whitewashed cottage with a thick thatched roof. Before Ben (as I came to know him) had time to usher me out of the car, the door in the middle of the cottage was opened and, standing on the threshold, was a woman of late middle age with curled, greying hair and lustrous, golden-brown eyes. I felt momentarily aggrieved that Peter's description of his stepmother, Grace, had left me unprepared for the elegant and lovely woman who was now welcoming me. I was glad, however, that I had decided to dress in what I thought to be an appropriately restrained style for this occasion: a silky, navy blue dress embellished with a white lace collar that brother Joe had sent me from wartime Malta.

Inside Rose Cottage a strangely ceremonial exchange of greetings took place between Ben, Grace and me, during which Peter stood by, unusually subdued and silent. Immediately enchanted by what I saw, I enthused about everything – first, the low-ceilinged dining-room with its polished oak furniture and brasses, then the sitting-room with its faded, chintz-covered chesterfield, and beside it a small round table on which stood a huge bowl of mixed coloured sweet peas which filled the cottage with their scent. As I enthused, Grace interjected a more or less constant stream of apologies or complaints about the smallness of the rooms, the lowness of the ceilings and – to her greatest embarrassment – the lack of facilities. And all the while Ben joined in with joking asides

to me, alternately bristling at his wife's complaints or trying
to console or reassure her.

It was true that modern facilities in the cottage were lack-
ing. There was electric light, but no bathroom or piped water
upstairs; and the kitchen was little more than a scullery at
the bottom of dark, narrow stairs leading up to the two small
bedrooms under the eaves. But worst of all to Grace was
that the lavatory was a wooden-seated closet at the bottom
of the garden. It did not seem to help Grace that with Ben's
help everything both inside and outside seemed to me to be
lovely. In the morning, Ben brought me heated-up rain-water
in a shining brass can to use in the rosewood wash-stand
with its bowl and jug of Doulton blue china. The walk down
the beautiful garden where huge delphiniums were almost in
flower in the long herbaceous border at the side of the lawn
was a delight. And it was no hardship to sit in the whitewashed privy in which the wooden bench seat had been
scrubbed to a bonelike yellow by Ben's daily ministrations.

What was not so enjoyable were the mealtimes. Grace was
an excellent cook and talented flower arranger. The table –
laid by Ben – gleamed with the silver-plate cutlery, fine table
linen, china and glassware which, like a lot of their things,
had come down to them from their families. But by the end
of each meal my head would be spinning from the stress of
polite conversation (politics were forbidden as unsuitable)
interspersed with the bickering between Ben and Grace that
seemed to be a compulsive picking of emotional scabs. Ben's
over-zealous concern that I had all I needed was also unnerving
as he bobbed up and down removing a plate, pouring water,
or urging second helpings on me I did not want. It made a
strange comparison with the behaviour at mealtimes with which
I was familiar at home and where, except at weekends, silence
was more common than either conversation or bickering.

At some point before the weekend was over, I found myself alone with Ben in the sitting-room, seated beside him
on the chesterfield. To my astonishment, Ben cut himself
short on one of the trivial anecdotes that he considered to
be an essential oil of civilized behaviour and took my hand
in his. 'I want you,' he said, 'to promise me that you will
stick by Peter. He was so young when he lost his mother,

and he has had his problems and been wild, but he is a good fellow really. What he needs is a lovely girl like you to keep him on the rails.' The character he had given his son did not seem to me either accurate or of a kind likely to encourage me to commit myself to Peter if – unbeknown though this was to Ben – I had not done so already. It was hard for me to restrain my instant reaction of indignation at this uncalled-for plea, based, as I saw it, on a mixture of flattery of me and denigration, if muted, of my beloved. I pulled away my hand and, laughing with embarrassment, said, 'Oh, I can't promise anything, but I'll try.' I was cross, but not enough to want to hurt the feelings of this kindly man. Whatever lay behind the middling reference he had given his son, I sensed that, like me, he loved Peter.

Leaving us at the station at the end of our brief visit, Ben squeezed my hand once more and said, 'Please try to do what I asked.' (My God, I thought, does he really believe I should take his son out of pity?)

'What was all that about?' asked Peter when we had settled into our seats and were on our way back to London. I told him. 'Oh, that'll be Grace nagging Ben to say something,' he said. Then after a slight pause he added laconically, 'You made a great impression. Ben's a snob, but she's even worse. She'd love to have a "lady almoner" as a daughter-in-law and thinks you'd be a great catch for me.'

It was an evening when Peter was on duty at the Hungerford that he rang me, as he usually did when nothing much was happening. 'Are you still prepared to go ahead with this marrying?' he asked. 'Because if you are, I'm going to arrange it. I could ask Donald Soper to marry us. I think he would agree.' He did agree, but only after he had interviewed us. 'It is a great responsibility, marrying people,' he said, perhaps sensing my resentment at what I saw as his unnecessary questions on our wanting to marry.

I was not prepared either for Mum's reaction when I broke the news to her, which I did when I got home one evening as we were washing up in the kitchen. Far from looking pleased or offering congratulations, she looked dismayed. 'But why?'

she cried. 'Why him? He's got nothing.' This brought cousin Ken in from the living-room to see what was up. Disappointed as I was at her dismay, I tried to explain. 'Well, yes. But he's going to go to Oxford, and. . . .' Mum cut me short. 'To be a student!' she said, the contempt in her voice displacing the dismay. Doing his best to help, Ken dropped his voice low and, putting his arm round Mum's shoulders, growled quietly, 'I expect she knows what she's doing.' I must have been in a very good mood myself, for I tried again to help Mum see her error. 'But don't you see, if I was going to marry someone who's got a £1,000 a year, like Rose has, he'd have to be about forty.' Mum's voice rose higher: 'But you *haven't even looked*!' she howled.

The day was fixed for Saturday, 31 July 1948. Following came the August Bank Holiday Monday, which meant that we could have a brief honeymoon over the long weekend. I was still working at Hammersmith Hospital and Miss Warren had to be given the news. As I was her student, she considered my welfare was her concern, and this meant yet another interview. Her shrewd grey eyes scanned my face as she asked me how long I had known this man, what he did and where he was heading in life. As I had often observed in her interviews with patients, she inspired confidence, and I found myself giving a fulsome description of Peter. 'So you feel sure that his plans for your future are realistic?' she asked in her fluty but matter-of-fact voice. 'Well yes,' I blurted out. 'You see, although you could say his head is in the clouds, his feet are on the ground.'

Three days before the wedding-day, the telephone on Miss Oswald's desk rang as, of course, it often did. On this occasion after she had picked it up she looked across at me and said disapprovingly, 'It's a man, for you.' Students were not meant to accept calls, and I gave what I hoped was a look combining apology and mystification as she passed the receiver to me. It was Philippe. 'How on earth did you get hold of this number?' I asked, only too conscious of Miss Oswald's attentive ears. Ignoring my question, Philippe said, 'We must meet. When can I see you?' 'I can't see you,' I said, adding hastily as I saw Miss Oswald's eyes widening, 'I must go.' He was not to be dismissed so easily – as I knew too well. There was nothing for it but to silence him with the truth. 'I can't see you again. I'm getting married on Saturday.'

10

To Have and to Hold

At home, the atmosphere did not improve when I tried to explain that Peter and I intended to get married with 'no fuss', and that neither my family nor Peter's were expected to take part. In fact, the atmosphere grew so gloomy and oppressive I had reluctantly to agree that Dad and Mum could come if they must. Peter's parents, who were more polite, less determined and not near enough to lean on us, accepted our edict without protest. For this I was thankful. I didn't want Ben and Grace looking down their noses at my family and so risk losing the high standing I seemed to have acquired in the eyes of the snobbish Grace.

Luckily, Pat and Frank were going on holiday and had asked me if I wanted to use their flat, as I had done before when they went away. It was to be for the whole fortnight before the day I was to get married. It meant that I could avoid, as much as possible, Mum's long face at this awkward time. One disadvantage, though, was that Frank made it quite clear he did not want me causing gossip, and what Frank called my 'men friends' were not included in the invitation to stay at the flat. Peter thought this ridiculously stuffy and not something that Frank could possibly have meant to be taken seriously. But I knew Frank better. I saw Frank's stiff code of honour as simply part of the person whom I loved and admired and I knew that to ignore his wishes would be, in his eyes, a betrayal of his trust. But sticking to his rules did mean that, hungry as Peter and I were for each other, love-making in the flat was forbidden.

There was still Peter's room at the Hungerford, and it was there we went together for the last time before we were to marry. We got there at the end of an exhausting Saturday afternoon, during which we had walked from one end to the other of Oxford Street trying to find a hat for me to wear for the wedding. Only at the very last moment did we find one on which we could agree. It was disconcerting, even a bit worrying, to discover that once again our taste over my clothes was proving to be so different. We managed to compromise, rather than agree, on a pale pink felt with a flat crown, a narrow brim, and trimmed with a minute fringe of dotted net. I planned to wear it with my green gaberdine suit – something else Peter had never liked because of its padded, rather military-looking shoulders. In my limited wardrobe, it was the one fairly suitable garment I could produce (in contrast to Peter's smart new coffee-coloured, herring-bone suit, which he had bought at Simpson's for the occasion).

On the morning of the wedding, I travelled up from the flat on the top deck of a bus. Meg, who had stayed the night at East Sheen, was with me. Hard up, and also ham-strung by clothes rationing, Meg had warned me that she had nothing very suitable to wear. Even so, to my slight alarm, I found that she looked more bridelike than I did in a flower bestrewn straw hat she had borrowed from her sister, and a dress of pink and blue floral cotton with a triple-tiered, flounced skirt. We got off the bus at a stop only yards from the Strand Palace Hotel. But on this fresh July morning my thoughts were entirely focused on the present moment and not at all on how differently the year had begun for me on New Year's Day.

In the few months since Peter and I had met, Meg and her boy-friend, Jake, had become as much Peter's friends as mine, and it was they who were to be our two witnesses. It took only a few minutes for Meg and me to reach Kingsway Hall, having dawdled a little so as to arrive exactly at the time we had agreed to meet Peter and Jake. They were not there, but Mum and Dad were – along with Wal, Pete, Joe and Ken, looking strangely stiff in their demob suits – and the porch of Kingsway Hall seemed to be full of my family. I gave what must have been a rather strained smile and said as carelessly as I could manage, 'Where's Peter?' 'Not here,' said Mum smugly. To which the only possible reply had to be a light-hearted 'Oh, I expect he'll turn up.' Indeed, I had no doubt that he would turn up, but I was put out. Luckily, Meg soon eased the slightly chilly atmosphere. She had always been a great favourite with my parents, as well as my brothers, and on greeting her they brightened up.

A minute or two later my apologetic groom arrived with Jake, and our small party made its way into the little chapel inside Kingsway Hall. Peter and I went in hand in hand (shocking one of the church helpers, we were told later, by this unconventional behaviour). Standing beside Peter at the altar rail, I could sense the weighty presence of my family behind me and I felt grateful that Meg and Jake had tactfully sat down behind Peter. Then I forgot all of them as Donald Soper, dignified and solemn in dog-collar and cassock, began to intone in his mellifluous voice the historic prose poem of the marriage service. He rounded off the ceremony with a blessing full of hope for a 'fruitful partnership of love and work for this young couple'. I looked up at Peter and smiled. He smiled back, and as if by magic a shaft of radiant sunlight came from somewhere above and shone down on us.

This moment of magic was rapidly dispelled when we moved to the vestry to sign the register and I found Dad standing behind me. It emerged that he was not to be prevented by the quixotic ideas of his only daughter from playing at least some role at her marriage. He pushed forward, determined to be one of the witnesses and managed to press his claim in place of Meg. As he leant towards the desk to sign, a strong smell of whisky wafted over all of us. For an awful moment I wondered if Dr Soper, who was known to be a convinced teetotaller, might feel obliged to interrupt his work on the marriage certificate to lecture Dad on the evils of drink.

It must be rare to have no photographs of one's wedding, but I am relieved that I have none of me in that stiff green suit and compromise pink hat. Joe and Ken, both keen photographers, had brought their cameras with them but, disconcerted by the austere, secular ambience, they did not use them. With Dad impatient to celebrate his small victory as much as the ceremony, we were hurried off to find a pub round the corner. Again, this was not what I had intended for this special day in my life, and in the few yards between chapel and pub I managed to make clear to Peter that we need only stay for one drink.

Leaving my family to share their celebrations with just Meg and Jake, Peter and I gave as our excuse for hurrying away so quickly that we had a train to catch for our secret honeymoon destination. Since we were going no further than to the village of Westerham in Kent, we could have walked the short distance to Charing Cross Station; but impetuously Peter hailed a passing taxi, which added a dash of luxury to our getaway. Excited and happy, we agreed that Donald Soper's little eulogy had surely been tailored specially for us, and had expressed just what we hoped for our future; and on the train Peter told me how Dad had taken him aside and said gruffly, 'She's a good girl, Pete. Look after her.'

We had booked a room for two nights at the King's Arms in Westerham. It was an attractive, red-tiled old inn, with timbered walls outside and cosy, with low ceilings, inside. Window-boxes were bright with red geraniums and the one on the sill of our bedroom window added to the charm of the room's white walls, blue curtains and simple furniture. For our first night together I had brought with me an ankle-length nightdress I had had made from a length of reject (or possibly black market) parachute nylon I'd acquired from somewhere during the war. Silky white, soft and voluminous it was more pretty than practical. In any case, it was not the stimulus to the night of passion I had expected. Unforeseen staffing problems at the Hungerford just before the Bank Holiday weekend had meant that Peter had been on night duty before the wedding and had had little sleep in the preceding forty-eight hours. Over our dinner at the King's Arms he was unusually subdued, and by the time we got into bed, other than saying that he could barely keep awake, he seemed unwilling to talk at all. To my dismay he was soon asleep, lying in my arms more like a child than either husband or lover.

Carefully extricating myself (no easy task with the voluminous nightdress) I got out of bed and, feeling strangely wraith-like, crossed the room to the window. Looking out over the geraniums and across the wide, half-lit street I listened for a while to the sound of dance music floating across from somewhere opposite. This, I thought, is surely an odd and lonely start to a marriage – and then I remembered the story of the parents of a friend I had got to know while in remote north Norfolk during my WAAF days in the war. The story was that the groom had been perfectly charming and normal until the day of the wedding, but had never spoken to his wife in all the years after it. For an unnerving moment I wondered if this might be my fate too. After all, I had met this man I had just married barely four months ago: how could I be sure that I really knew him? I got back into bed and looked down at this fair-skinned stranger, breathing so steadily, and looking in sleep so remote, so young and vulnerable. My thoughts went back through the day, until I was again standing there beside Peter in the shaft of sunlight, while well-known phrases – 'To have and to hold', 'For better or for worse' – echoed in my head.

Next morning, Peter was back to his usual, confident and extrovert self. Although we loved and lazed away much of the day on the grassy, meadowy hills just outside the village, by the end of it we had decided not to stay a second night at the King's Arms. We were too impatient to get back to London and to our first home. The 'room of one's own' I had yearned for was, in the end, to be a bed-sitting-room for two.

It was Peter who had taken on the far from easy job of finding somewhere for us at a price we could afford. Before we were married we had gone to look at it together (and to be vetted by the landlord). Peter warned me that I might find it 'too small and dreary', but that it was the best he could find. It was a furnished room in a large house in Belsize Park that had seen grander days but was now split up into bed-sitters. When we arrived the landlord was waiting for us. He was a tall, stout man in a navy blue overcoat and dark-rimmed glasses. To Peter's surprise, when we had climbed the stairs and reached the first-floor landing, the landlord said, 'I want to show you this room first' – and unlocked the door of a room that was not at all 'small and dreary' as Peter had warned me to expect. It was large, high ceilinged and with a big square bay at one end with diamond-paned windows that looked out on to a lush, green garden below. There was a large, shabby carpet covering most of the floor with a smaller patterned rug on top of it at one end. Against the party wall were two single divans with cotton covers in a cottagey blue check. There was a gas fire and, in a corner behind a screen, a gas stove (with a small table beside it for pots and pans). An old-fashioned Edwardian wardrobe (with a door that did not quite shut) stood against the opposite wall and near it was a hand-basin, cracked at the bottom, but with hot and cold water taps. To us it seemed sumptuous.

'It's very nice,' said Peter, 'but surely this would cost a lot more than the one you showed me before?'

There was a slight hesitation before the landlord replied: 'No, no. You can have it for the same rent.'

We could hardly believe our luck; we knew that at £2 a week this really was a bargain.

I never saw the room we might have had because by the time we moved it had been let to someone else – a very quiet single man whose presence could sometimes be sensed, more than heard, through the connecting door concealed behind our wardrobe. His room had, we deduced, been the dressing-room in the grander days of the house's history. We liked to speculate on why we had been so lucky, why we had been favoured by the landlord. Was it, we wondered, that as young lovers about to marry we had touched a soft spot of romanticism in him?

After we had moved our single beds to be close against each other (so that we could still hold hands when we at last settled down to sleep), we invented another even less probable reason for the landlord's beneficence. Moving the beds inspired us to look for a new position for the loose rug, but when we took it up we discovered why it was there. On the worn carpet underneath was a darkly sinister-looking stain. It was as big as a manhole. What could have caused such a large and apparently irremovable mark? we wondered. Could it be blood? Had someone committed suicide or been murdered in this lovely room? Could this be why the landlord had been so taken with us, feeling that we might, through our obvious happiness, exorcise something bad that had happened in the past? We put the rug back where it was. It was a past that had nothing to do with us and should not be allowed to spoil our joy in this our first home.

After the honeymoon weekend, I went back to Hammersmith Hospital and Peter to the Hungerford. On weekday
evenings we concocted together some sort of meal on the
gas stove, and it was pleasant to sit at the table by the bay
window and eat looking out on to the garden. It was one
weekend morning when the smell of the bacon I was cooking for my breakfast persuaded Peter that he was, after all,
not at heart a vegetarian. And at breakfast too that I found
I had really shocked Peter by absent-mindedly licking my
knife. From hurt pride, I accused him of being just as bound
by petty convention as his parents. Peter knew enough about
my past to understand my furious reaction, but he was probably less aware – as I was myself then – just how much this
was based on my own unease about social class.

Most of the time just being together was perfect happiness; absorbed in each other, we neglected relatives and friends.
Whether we were quietly studying, reading or going to the
cinema, shopping together or walking on Hampstead Heath,
we hated to be separated, and we weren't – apart from the
occasional evening when Peter had to go alone to meet Derek
Pont, a close friend of his, in a pub. To his disappointment,
Peter found that, whereas to him pubs were 'interesting social institutions' to be enjoyed with a decent glass of bitter
and the chance to observe mankind, to me they spelt lower-
class boredom. I much preferred that on a Friday or Saturday evening Meg and Jake should join us in our room. There,
with one – or at most two – bottles of cider to stimulate us,
we could pass the evening in lively discussions on the social
problems and political issues that interested all of us; and
end up in merriment or torpor in the early hours.

11
Frosty Morning

The weeks fled by and, as summer days shortened, papers began to arrive from Ruskin College about arrangements that must be made for Peter's first term as a student. My own brief days as student were drawing to an end. Kit Stewart had been warmly enthusiastic as always on hearing about my plans to marry. '*What* thrilling and lovely news,' she wrote in a letter sent two days before the wedding and with 'a tiny token' – a book about the faith of Edward Wilson, the Antarctic hero. 'I do *so* believe in marriage,' she went on. 'It must be the perfect maximum giving and receiving. I'm sure you're wise to marry now, but *so* glad you're finishing the training!'

I explained that I was not only going to finish but expecting to get a job afterwards, preferably in Oxford where Peter would be. She told me that she knew a vacancy at the Radcliffe Hospital had been filled only recently but, always wanting to help, suggested I should write anyway to inquire if another vacancy might be coming up. I wrote off at once, but a curt reply made clear that I would not be starting my career in hospital social work in Oxford. As October drew closer, and with it the prospect of being parted from Peter, I began to talk about getting some other work – anything, like serving in Woolworth's – to avoid our being separated. Peter would not agree. He believed (as at bottom I did too) that I ought to follow the career for which I had qualified, that I would not be happy if I did not do so, and that if I was not happy it would not be much of a help while he was studying to have me with him.

It occurred me that Peter's feet were even more firmly on the ground than I had perhaps realized when I gave my thumbnail sketch of his character to Miss Warren. He pointed out that there was a good coach service between Oxford and London and we should be able to meet most weekends in one place or the other. He was also sure that my work and his studies would help us to get through the days we were parted. What did worry him was that I might be lonely and miserable living on my own in Belsize Park, and it was this that led to the idea that we should move into some unfurnished rooms in Derek Pont's house on the edge of Canonbury.

The house, tall and narrow, was one of a pair that stood like two sharpened, up-ended pencils at the end of a row of grander Victorian villas in Northampton Park. Derek and his wife Rita had rented the house following the birth of their baby son. With no floor-covering at all on the steep stairs, and a high-ceilinged but bare hall, the house seemed at first sight pretty bleak. But when you entered the large double room off the hall, this first impression was soon dispelled. Made bright by the light pouring in from the window at each end, and Rita's colourful paintings pinned on the walls, it was almost empty of furniture. There was a low divan heavily draped with a cover of rich red, two shabby but ornate Victorian armchairs judiciously placed on the edges of a small rug in front of a fireplace, and a huge display of twigs in a vase in one corner. To live like this, I felt, would be just as attractively unconventional in its way as living in Hampstead.

The Ponts were hard pressed for money and, although they made clear they believed they were doing us a favour, were glad of the chance of some contribution towards the rent that subletting to us would offer. What they proposed was that we should rent, unfurnished, the two attic rooms under the pointed roof, and one of the two rooms in the basement, sharing the kitchen down there, as well as the one lavatory. With two floors between our rooms at the top of the house and the kitchen and lavatory at the bottom, the arrangement was not exactly convenient.

By the time Peter's term was about to begin, I still had no job, and this made the thought of his departure harder to bear, so I decided to book up to go potato picking for a fortnight on a farm just outside Oxford where we could be close to each other. Finding myself once more in a Nissen hut with a group of strangers, I froze the first night under one thin blanket – the others for my bed having been filched by those who had got to the hut earlier. Hunched up on my bed at the end of the interminable back-bending days of work that followed, I ruminated on the turn of events that had brought me here. This cold, inconvenient hut, the frosty early morning fields, canteen meals and carried mugs, all too reminiscent of my days in the WAAF – perhaps I'm now too old for this, I thought.

Walking about with Peter in Oxford, its quadrangles and river banks romantically melancholy in autumn colours, and going back for tea in his small but cosy bed-sit did not help. Feeling pushed out and on the edge of this beautiful charmed world, I realized what a mistake it had been to come. It was bad enough being left on my own, but hard as I tried I could not suppress feelings of envy and anger, knowing as I did the bleakness of the camp life to which I had to return. I had booked to stay for a fortnight, but at the end of the first miserable week I went back to London. One weekend soon after that, we left our room in Belsize Park – to the irritation of the landlord, whom we had clearly disappointed – and moved to Northampton Park.

With under £30 left of my diminishing demob gratuity we had to make do with what we could find in the way of furniture. Out and about on his building work, Dad picked up for our basement room a solid deal table with rounded corners, fat, square legs and a bare, scrubbed top. For her part, Mum offered us two upright carver chairs with brown rexine seats which she did not want, and which I did not much like but was glad to have for lack of anything better. For our attic room with its gabled ceiling Peter had found a couple of metal-framed beds at a junk-shop. With mattresses and covers these served as seats as well as beds, and we had also found (a bargain at 15 shillings) a pretty Georgian dressing-table in satinwood, which we used as a desk. Beside it, in the bookcase that my brother Joe had made me years ago and that I had had in my bedroom at Lee, we assembled our small joint library. But our great pride was our curtains of heavy Jacquard furnishing fabric bought in a sale in a large store we happened to be passing in City Road, near the Old Street underground station. The thick green fabric had a woven-in pattern of small, gold-coloured leaves and, in our eyes, furnished the room. Made up with Mum's help on her old sewing-machine, they hung, full and heavy, from ceiling level down to the black, stained floor-boards.

Although when I returned to London it was anguish to be apart from Peter, it was an anguish that only increased the fervour of our frequent reunions, whether in the home that delighted us or in Oxford. For the weekends in Oxford Miss Selby, Peter's spinsterish, gentle landlady in Walton Street, put up a narrow camp-bed for me beside Peter's not much wider – but certainly more comfortable – divan. Between our reunions, we would sometimes telephone each other, but conscious of expense (and also of being overheard by the Ponts or Miss Selby) we mostly wrote letters to keep in touch. Peter found out that if he caught the last post at midnight his letter would reach me by eight the next morning, and our letters flew back and forth almost daily.

Meanwhile, my efforts to find a job were not going well. At first, I enjoyed the sense of freedom; it was like being on a well-earned holiday after the fairly intensive year of study and I filled my time with what Mum called – this time re-provingly – 'gadding about'. I pointed out huffily that although no longer a student I was still preparing myself for my new career, and to confirm this I gave her a long description of the group visit to the Ford factory at Dagenham that Kit Stewart had arranged. Until then, I had never been inside a factory, and I was shocked by what I saw. 'The men have to shuffle on little stools alongside the moving belt, just to fit one screw or add on one bit of bodywork,' I told her. 'And there are things moving about in all directions above and around. And the noise! It's awful!' 'There you are, now you know how easy your life's been,' Mum said, which infuriated me. I knew she had never been inside a factory herself and I did not see why she should consider this a lesson just for me.

I did not tell her that my 'gadding about' also included another trip I had made on my own behalf. This was to the pioneering Marie Stopes birth control clinic in Whitfield Street and, in a different way, it proved to be even more of a shock to me than the Ford factory had been. One of the things that had impressed me when Peter and I first made love between his grey sheets at the Hungerford was the confident way that, at the right moment, he produced a condom. It would not be true to say that I had never seen one before, but I was certainly not familiar with them. I soon discovered that for me condoms and passion were not compatible; to put it bluntly, I did not like them. Sensibly, Peter pointed out that, if condoms were so unacceptable to me, 'being careful' hard on both of us, and pregnancy something we hoped to defer, we had to find a better way.

In the romantic adventures I had indulged in before I met Peter I had always feared, but mainly through good luck escaped, getting pregnant. In his entanglements Peter had been less fortunate. He knew that getting an unwanted pregnancy aborted, at a time when (and for another twenty years) this was illegal, was a traumatic and sordid experience.

In 1948 family planning was still a very private matter, and for many – perhaps most – people, birth control (as it was then more commonly called) was an embarrassing topic. Birth control clinics were few and far between, and strictly reserved for bona fide married women. So it was very nervously, and with some reluctance, that I went along one sunny afternoon to Whitfield Street, walking up and down outside the clinic until I had the courage to go in. In a small, shabby waiting-room inside, a woman in a white overall was sitting at a desk. She looked at me severely and, I felt, suspiciously – a feeling that was confirmed when I sat down opposite her and she began to question me. I don't think she actually asked if I had brought my marriage certificate with me (which I had not), but I felt that she was seeking this sort of proof of my credentials. Even when she did decide that I could be helped, she was brusque. 'You'll have to be examined by the doctor. You can't see her today. You'll have to come back.' Angry at her patronizing manner, humiliated by her questioning, I gritted my teeth, nodded, got up and left. I had no intention of ever going back.

At Northampton Park I did not have much to do with Derek or Rita, who were both too absorbed in their launch into parenthood to want to spend time with old friends, let alone

making a new one of me. But I had my own friends to turn
to, like Ann and Meg, whom I enjoyed entertaining in my
own part of the house. I saw more of Meg because she too
had a gap in life. Jake had successfully gained a place under
the ex-servicemen's resettlement scheme at Balliol and, only
a week or two after Peter had left for Oxford, the Michaelmas
term had begun and Jake had gone up too. He and Peter
had soon got together over tea in Jake's college room, on
walks along the banks of the Thames or the canal, or over
pints of beer in one of the many Oxford pubs, cementing
their friendship in prolonged debates on politics and litera-
ture (or what Peter in frivolous mood delighted in calling
'the eternal trivialities').

Meg and I were more interested in the practical problems
of social policy. Half-way through her studies for a social
science diploma Meg was now in her second year at Bedford
College. It meant that, through her, I could still sometimes
vicariously enjoy student life, going along with her to public
lectures, or lounging in the pleasant grounds of the college
in Regent's Park with her and her friends. Meg for her part
enjoyed coming to stay with me at Northampton Park because it gave her a break from being back at home with her
parents. As a VAD in the war years, Meg had left home, but
partly through lack of money, and partly because her parents
expected it, she had had to go back to live with them and
that was not always easy.

The leaves were falling faster, the days getting shorter and
sometimes foggy, and I was still unemployed. Time began to
hang a little more heavily and forced me to mull over what
I was up to and where I was going. 'I'm still living on capital – lit[erally] and fig[uratively],' I scribbled in my journal
in early November. 'After another wonderful weekend how
can I be expected to come out of my ambrosiac [*sic*] world
down to earth? . . . Nevertheless my conscience niggles that
it's high time I began to pay my way in life . . . I would like
now to really pitch into a job – beginning next week. . . .
Mum suggested today that Peter would settle to the weekend routine more easily if he knew I was at work all week
and not "gadding about". As usual there is a grain of truth
in what she says.'

12

What Giving Really Means

Hackney Hospital, a former public assistance infirmary, was in those days a wholly grim collection of looming rectangular brick buildings set back behind a high wall on Homerton High Street. On the right-hand side of the gatehouse entrance, male staff in a porter's lodge saw in the ambulances and directed the new arrivals, patients and visitors. I was sent over to the opposite side of the gatehouse where the clerical staff of the Almoners' Department and its head, Miss Shorey, had their offices.

Miss Shorey, a small, neatly built woman, had her dark hair drawn into a bun, and there was the hint of the same dark hair on her upper lip. Her white coat-overall was spotless, and her manner matter-of-fact to the point of brusqueness. She introduced me to her deputy, a large, full-breasted, clumsy-looking woman in wire-framed glasses. She too was in a white coat, but even so looked more like an overgrown Girl Guider, which in fact she turned out to be. After a brief interview, Miss Shorey took me on a tour of the hospital. Its gloomy blocks and long, bleak wards did nothing to raise my spirits at the prospect of working here if the job were offered to me – as it was.

Each day in the afternoon the staff of the Almoners' Department met in the general office by the gatehouse where Miss Shorey would join us as we chatted over our cups of tea. It was there that I got to know another member of the almoning staff who seemed both friendly and closer to me in age and opinions. In those more formal days, staff normally did not use first names, but Daphne and I soon did. She was a pretty young woman with fluffy, light-brown hair and green eyes. Even more unusual about her eyes than their colour was that the left one turned slightly outwards and gave her an expression of scanning alertness.

At the end of the day Daphne and I would often leave together and, engrossed in discussion on our present work and future career prospects, would walk back up Homerton High Street, across the churchyard and past the remains of the old parish church to pick up our buses in Mare Street. At that time, long before the Clean Air Act, acrid, eye-stinging, throat-tickling 'pea soup' fogs could close in and cause havoc from autumn onwards. On one occasion, the fog was so dense as we were going home that Daphne and I had to feel our way along, bumping into walls and tripping over kerbs like blind people, and having no idea where we were.

Having been disappointed in my hopes for a job at a more prestigious place such as St Thomas's, or at University College (where I had gone for an interview but not been selected), I had started work at Hackney as a locum in the middle of November. In the end as the weeks went by without my finding a place, I was glad to accept the position, knowing that if something better did not turn up there was a chance that the temporary post could become a permanent one.

Facing the gatehouse buildings in which I had been interviewed by Miss Shorey, and across a small courtyard, were what had been the impressive quarters of the former Board of Guardians before the post-war reforms to create the Welfare State had finally extinguished the old Poor Law. A small ante-room, used as a waiting-room, led into the former boardroom built for the Guardians. With its high ceilings, grand carved fireplace at one end, three large windows along one side, highly polished parquet floor and shining brass trimmings to cupboards and doors, it made an imposing office, now turned over to the Almoners' Department. In this huge room, and set at right angles to the first window at one end of it, was my desk. Close to the ornate fireplace at the far end was the desk of the maternity almoner, Miss Spink, a woman whom I instantly disliked and found fussy and spinsterish, and who obviously felt a similar antipathy towards me. Although we faced each other when sitting at our desks, because the room was so large we were luckily still quite far apart; and as we were looking after different wards and patients, we did not need to have much to do with each other except over claims on our shared clerk, who had a desk half-way between us.

Before the National Health Service had begun six months earlier, famed voluntary hospitals such as St Thomas's had administered their own schemes for getting contributions towards the cost of treatment from their patients – including the rattling of tins (as I had found out while in the Casualty Department at St Thomas's). In earlier times, when they were first employed in hospitals, most almoners had been called on to carry out some financial assessment of what patients could pay, and made the arrangements for patients needing convalescence, transport or surgical appliances. But increasingly it came to be seen that their training as medical social workers had qualified them to help with the more complex social and personal problems that ill-health, disablement and old age tend to bring.

In some more progressive hospitals, even before the NHS had begun, almoners had stopped dealing with financial assessment and similar time-consuming tasks, and saw patients and their families only when these were referred to them by medical or nursing staff who thought help was needed with more complex problems. At Hackney where, as elsewhere, financial assessment was no longer needed, and where the almoners' clerks dealt with transport needs and the simpler practical problems, Miss Shorey had ruled (in consultation with the hospital's Medical Director) that every in-patient must still be seen so that, whatever the problem, patients coming into or going out of hospital could be offered help if necessary.

As one of the almoners with several wards to look after, I had plenty to keep me busy, for along with seeing all the patients coming into the medical wards for which I had responsibility, there was the resulting work I had to do at my desk in the former boardroom. There were case-notes to be written so that when staff had left, or were temporarily absent, patients and relatives did not have to be asked again for details they had already given. Telephone calls had to be made to arrange home helps for the old or sick. Inquiries had to be made or letters written about convalescence, patients' housing, money difficulties and other problems, and relatives of patients had sometimes to be seen.

Miss Shorey, unlike some of the more eminent members of the medical social work profession, believed that simple practical problems of transport, convalescence and arrangements for surgical aids were still among the tasks with which she (and her clerical staff) should be concerned. It was a view I partly shared, although at the same time I was convinced that to help with personal and emotional difficulties was equally – sometimes more – important.

At Hammersmith Hospital I had learnt a series of questions about sickness benefit and domestic problems which I usually went through, and which had the additional underlying aim of establishing an initial rapport with patients. To begin an interview with a patient by asking 'Are the family managing all right without you?' seemed sensible; whereas to appear at the bedside of someone to whom you were a complete stranger and start off by asking 'Are you having difficulties with your sex life?' did not.

Too soon I got into a routine with these opening questions, and having found out from one man who had come into hospital with a suspected gastric ulcer that he had received his sickness benefit, I murmured almost automatically, 'Good'. Was he married? I went on and, hearing another 'Yes', again I murmured 'Good'. The trouble came when in answer to my next question – 'Any children?' – he said 'No', and yet another 'Good' popped out from me. 'What do you mean, "Good"?' the poor man said indignantly. 'It isn't good at all – my wife and I have been trying for six years!'

I can never forget and still find painful to recall another more serious mistake I made. It happened when one day Dr Poulton, one of the paediatricians, came in to tell me that he had a patient – a nine-year-old girl – about whom there was some concern. The child had been admitted several times in recent months, and each time she came in her hair was matted and infested with nits. Although always sent home in a clean condition from the hospital, she invariably was in just as bad a state next time she was admitted. When I went to see Sister on the Children's Ward she took me along to meet little Jenny. She had dark, thick hair brushed back from her face, black eyes and a skin almost as white as the stiff hospital nightdress she was wearing. Sister and I agreed that she would make sure that the mother came to see me next time she visited. In fact she did not turn up then but, after Sister had exerted further strong pressure, she arrived a day or two later. I knew as this woman – a small, bedraggled creature – came through the door that I was about to face a sticky situation when I saw she was not alone. She had brought her husband with her, a tall, round-shouldered man with a defensively sullen expression.

At my invitation both sat down, the wife looking nervous, the husband suspicious. I began to explain gingerly that I had asked them to call because Sister was concerned about Jenny, and even more gingerly went on to skirt round the question of how it was that every time she was discharged from hospital her hair was quite clean, but each time she was readmitted it was infested and matted. The parents vied with each other in their emphatic protests that this was a problem for them too. The trouble was, they said, that their daughter had such naturally tight curling hair that, no matter what they did, it got tangled up. Moreover, when they tried to comb it, the girl made such a fuss that they had to stop; and the nits were not their fault either because, as everyone knows, they were picked up at school. My common sense told me that these were not very convincing excuses, but with little experience of looking after children I lacked the confidence to challenge the defences of these parents.

By bad luck my colleague, Miss Spink, had been at her desk and listening avidly during this sorry exchange, and as the parents closed the door behind them she said waspishly, 'They were talking nonsense. No child whose hair is combed and brushed properly could get into that condition.' It was bad enough to feel that she must be right. Much worse was the suspicion that this was not simply a case of neglected hair, but of a badly neglected child. Soon after, when the NSPCC rang to ask what I knew about the child, the suspicion was confirmed.

When I confessed this failure to Daphne, she urged me not to blame myself too much. With such problems it was easy to criticize, either for 'interfering' too soon and too much or for doing too little too late. Even social workers with years of experience, she pointed out, found it difficult to know what to do for the best when a child's welfare was at stake. It is one of the hardest dilemmas that social workers have to face, and finding the answer is no more easy today than it was then.

Happily, on many days – as surely it is for anyone who works in a hospital – it was possible, at least in a small way, to help patients and their relatives. It was on one such day that Amy, the clerk I shared with the prissy Miss Spink, said to me when I returned from one of my wards, 'Sister A2 rang down. She's got an old lady who is worrying about her husband, and would you see her as soon as you can.' A little later, on my way to A2 Ward, I passed through the waiting-room. It was a rather dark place, and for a moment it seemed to be empty until an elderly man jumped up from the gloom and stopped me. 'How much longer do I have to wait here?' he demanded aggressively. 'Who are you waiting to see?' I asked. 'They told me the medical secretary's office,' he said, adding miserably and as if it were almost shameful, 'It's for a death certificate. I knocked on that door, and some young girl told me to wait.'

Not for the first time in the few weeks I had been working at the hospital, I thought how sad it was that people must wait like this while hospital staff bustled about unnoticing. I remembered an earlier occasion when a horrendous keening had come from this same ante-room from a woman distraught with grief. The disturbing howls soon had people running in to take notice, but this poor man who had sat waiting quietly got no attention until anger made him hit out at the first passing figure – which happened to be me. I said sympathetically, 'I know they sometimes do keep you waiting so long. They are very busy, but you must knock again if they don't see you soon.' It was not much of a help, but enough. 'My wife died here yesterday,' the man said sadly. 'I don't know where I am.'

I had to hurry off. I could see that a crowd had gathered outside the closed iron gate across the courtyard. I needed to be quick to see the old lady on Ward A2 before the visitors were allowed in. But as I cut through the corridors –

dreary still, despite bright new paint – my thoughts were locked on the man in the ante-room. I said to myself, 'I'll go and chivvy them up if he's still there when I get back.'

'Bed eighteen. Her husband's ill, I think,' said Sister, rushing by. A tired-looking old woman, her shrunken body hunched up high in the bed, looked up at me. Her faded, wrinkled face was tight with anxiety. Confused and perhaps a little deaf, she found it difficult at first to understand who I was, what I was saying or how I differed from all the other white-coated figures who had come and gone by her bedside. But she came to life and was quick to respond when I asked about her husband. 'My daughter is looking after him,' she said, adding anxiously, 'Why? Is something the matter?' She gave a wan smile when I said I should like to see her daughter, and she promised she would not forget to tell her to come after visiting-time. I left a message with Sister, in case she did forget.

The bereaved man had gone from the waiting-room by the time I returned there. He would now be on his way to the next official – the registrar, the insurance man, the undertaker – I thought ruefully as I went into my office, knowing that before long the ante-room would be filling up with patients' relatives who needed to see me or Miss Spink.

Soon the first knock came. The afternoon was under way. A woman with a brown coat was about the fourth to come in. She was small, but I realized how small only when I stood up to greet her. She was perhaps forty, but her rosy cheeks and bright manner gave her a youthful air that contrasted strangely with her drab, shabby clothes. This was Miss Benny who was, I found out, the eldest child and the only unmarried daughter of the old lady I had seen in Ward A2. 'Mum hasn't been well for a long time now,' she told me. 'Then there's Dad . . . I don't know really who needs looking after most.' She explained that her father had been a semi-invalid for years and that, although he was no worse than usual, now that her mother's health was failing, she had recently had to give up work to cope with caring for both of them.

Not wanting to take up my time, as she said brightly, she got up to leave just as I asked: 'Will your job be open to you if and when you can go back?'

Her brightness diminished visibly. 'Well, I expect I *could* go back,' she said doubtfully, 'but I don't see how I can. . . .' Her voice trailed away into silence.

'That means you'll have to manage without your wages. Are you getting unemployment benefit?'

Miss Benny sat down again. It was already difficult. It was not the cleaning and the cooking and the caring; she had always been used to that sort of work. No, it was not that she minded, and as the only unmarried child of parents who had had a hard life bringing up a large family, it was no more than she should do for them now that they were old. No, the trouble was the money, because in the sort of work she had done she had never paid any National Insurance contributions. Trying to make the pensions, hardly adequate for two, enough for three – that was the problem.

It took some time to persuade her that the days of the Poor Law and public assistance were past that, she – and probably her parents as well – would be able to get some financial help under the new scheme of national assistance benefits, and that she did not even need to go to the office of the National Assistance Board to find out about this, as I could arrange for a 'visiting officer' to call on her at home.

Convinced at last, Miss Benny got up again, and this time she held out her hand, an unusual gesture for a woman in those days, which seemed almost mannish. It was a shock when our hands met. Against mine, this small woman's hand was not only big but as rough as glass-paper. At that moment the life of the woman came home to me, a life counted out, not in coffee-spoons but in buckets of cold water and harsh soda and soap and endless scrubbing of clothes and floors. Yet as her hand scratched mine, it flashed through my mind that really she might also be having a sort of revenge, that she was saying wordlessly: 'You with your helping and being thanked! Take this, and understand what giving really means.'

In spite of the sadness and poignancy, it was on one of these days that I went home to write in my journal: 'A good day at Hackney. Problems all day – all fascinating, some difficult. I tried hard to clear my desk before I left, but even by then had not succeeded.'

13
Birthmarks

Journal, 30 November 1948
This seems an odd way of living. Working in that gaunt
hospital all day, coming home to this quiet and aloneness
at night – and day after day mist and fog in the air all
adding to the feeling of unreality. This is not unhappiness
but the worrying confusion and wrongness of dreams.

Victor Silvester plays a tune on the radio. I find I
listen more to the radio these days. Or, rather, have it
on more often but listen less. At this moment, and in a
flash, and with wonderful relief, I'm back to Belsize
Park, then the little Everyman picture-house and Peter
and I, electrically alive, in the queue. Even inside, and
watching the *Blue Angel* – a passive enough state – there
was still the livingness, a constant dazzling inner light.

On top of this, is it possible I can be pregnant? Belief
says not, but Reason, yes. And there is no doubt now
that when and if all of me believes it I shall be panic-
stricken. Of course, I want children, *our* children; but I
know now that I do not want them yet. In the first
place I do not feel Peter or I have reached a stage in
our union to really understand or appreciate such a step.
No doubt a year after marriage is suitable for some, but
not for us.

The lack of money terrifies me. None now is one
thing, we have – to use one of Mum's boring old
phrases – 'only ourselves to please', and we are content
to be doing that. I think how I have inwardly criticized
Rita with her dowdy clothes, dirty shoes, horrid baby
clothes. And now I wonder how without money anyone
can be different.

99

In the sort of novels I read in my teens husbands, when told that their wives were pregnant, were invariably astonished. This had never seemed convincing to me, but the irony was that when Peter first suggested one Oxford weekend that I was pregnant, I was the one who was taken aback. By the time the term was drawing to an end I had found out that he was right.

Mon. 12 December 1948
I hope I shall not be feeling like this very often in the future. Such peculiar puffiness in the head; such horrible waving and unbalancing nausea. I resent such feelings, they seem unnatural. But then perhaps it is natural for a body undergoing such overwhelmingly important changes to make some complaint if too much other strain is brought to bear.

There was no doubt, in my mind, of the strain. I was bowled over by this threatening turn of events; so much so that my memories of the next few months are no more than a jumbled blur, and the pages of my journal mostly blank. With some reluctance I broke the news to the Ponts, who did their best to conceal their obvious dismay. Signs of strain between Rita and me over the shared parts of the house had already emerged, and the Ponts rightly foresaw that with another baby around the stresses would increase.

A weekend at Great Chesterford just before Christmas enabled Peter to break the news to Ben and Grace. Ben, always more concerned to be polite than honest, offered us his warm congratulations. In contrast, Grace made no attempt to hide her disapproval or that she placed the whole blame on her stepson-cum-nephew. In her eyes, it was yet further evidence of Peter's lack of any sense of responsibility. Having by guile or good fortune managed to capture this attractive and socially acceptable young woman, as she saw it, he had yet again proved his undependability. Indignant on behalf of my love, I insisted that neither Peter nor I had any doubts about each other or our future – aware as I was that at least the first part of this claim was wholly true.

As well as these depressing reactions, there was also that

of my mother, which, for me, was by far the hardest to put up with. It was only with the greatest reluctance that I got round to telling her, and when I did she said with infuriating complacency that she knew already. Whether or not this was so, I had long known that she had some queer theory that 'You can always tell in the first few weeks that a woman's pregnant from a pinched look round the nose'! What was even harder to bear when I told her was the look on her face which, as so often, revealed far more than her words. I knew that she was thinking, There you are! Going to be so clever, weren't you, Madam, but now you're trapped, just like I was. Just like all women are. What she said was not much better: 'Well, you'll have to start knitting, then. And what's Peter going to do? Will he get a job?'

It was the question that we had to face, and inevitably discussed a lot over the Christmas break. Once over the unpleasant early feelings of nausea, I was convinced that I could continue to work happily at Hackney Hospital until the last weeks of pregnancy. We knew that if I could do so, Peter would be able to stay on at Oxford until the end of his first year at Ruskin College, and then perhaps get a scholarship to continue his studies at the London School of Economics. But when the vacation was over and Peter had returned to Oxford his second letter revealed that, for him, what to do for the best was still far from clear.

'I've been feeling very miserable since I arrived,' he wrote. 'But I've just had a shave and I'm going to a meeting about community centres and I've talked myself into counting the days and cheering up a bit. I didn't like to express it yesterday but I know why I was miserable. I felt a failure, Poppet; not in my own estimation of my ability, but in my failure to manage the world well enough. . . . Then there was your talk of you working right to the end; which made me feel very responsible. But the fact that I'm able to write about it means that things are a little better. I've realized again that you love me as I love you and that *you* don't feel about things as *my* fault. Oh, I'll shut up now and just tell you again that we won't be apart much longer. It's wrong for us to be separated now.'

It dawned on me that Peter was just as conditioned by his

early experience in appropriate behaviour for husbands as I was in that for wives. What we intellectually regarded as outmoded ways were still speaking to both of us. It was what in my lighter moments I liked to call the 'silly old ghost voices' that were making Peter as uneasy about not taking care of me (as he had been reared to believe a husband should) as I was about wanting to reject the traditional roles of wife and mother.

Before Easter came round and another term had ended, Peter had made up his mind to leave Ruskin College. By then, despite my protestations that he ought at least to continue until the end of the first year, he was unshakeably convinced that he should be with me. He had made his plans and, in addition to his normal studies, was working hard for the scholarship to LSE in the hope that he could continue his studies there. But he had also begun to look for possible jobs in case the LSE plan failed.

This was how he happened to notice an item in the paper a few weeks before he was to rejoin me for good. 'Did you see a note about Michael Young in yesterday's *Observer*?' he asked in one of his letters posted at midnight in Oxford. 'He seems a good chap, right on the line, and I have thought that I might write to him, sending a sample of writing and asking about publicity work on neighbourhood activity. But I'm waiting to see a copy of his pamphlet *Small Man, Big World*.'

I think my ambivalent feelings about being pregnant finally vanished when some time in the spring I felt the baby quicken. By the time the hot days of summer had arrived I felt like a great swollen pod waiting to burst. I had gone on working as late as I could and, before I gave up, Peter had found a temporary office job. He was employed as a clerk in an income tax office, where he earned £5 a week. Later, he moved on to another temporary post in the St Pancras Electricity Company where he got £6 a week. Fortunately, I saw all this as no more than a transitory setback on our way to some as yet not very clear, but certainly bright, future. While Peter was still hoping that he would get a mature scholarship to go to the LSE, and a grant to go with it on which we could manage.

As the last weeks of my pregnancy dragged on, I spent a lot of my time once Peter had left for work reading in our attic bed-sitter or dreaming about what the future might have in store for us. We had got together a minimal sort of lay-ette, and found a second-hand pram of the kind – new then – that was basically a carry-cot on wheels. Made of a green waterproof fabric slung on a metal frame, it had no springs and looked what it was – well worn, second-hand.

Mum quickly gave up hope that I would apply myself to knitting, and set to work on behalf of 'this baby of yours', who would be her first grandchild. Whether I was visiting her in south-east London or she came to see me in Canonbury, her knitting would be with her, and soon brought out. If, over our cups of tea, we got on to my condition, I invari-ably ended up insisting that 'Things have changed since your time, Mum. These days, childbirth doesn't have to be pain-ful.' She would respond with an audible sniff, her brown eyes expressing scepticism.

Through my friend Ann Horton, early news of my preg-nancy had reached St Thomas's Hospital. 'How exciting. You must have the baby here,' wrote Maggie Mayfield, the ma-ternity almoner at Thomas's. She was a lively brunette whom I had got to know well as one of the course tutors during my training. She had just returned from a visit to the United States to see what medical social work was doing there and, thankfully, with her enthusiasm for life in general, she had none of the stuffiness of Miss Spink at Hackney Hospital.

After a bad night in late August (unhappily preceded by a domestic row with Rita over the use of the shared kitchen), I thought that my labour had started; and so in the early dawn of a fine clear morning Peter and I made our way by a bumpy ride on an almost empty tram to St Thomas's. Hav-ing settled me in there, Peter left for work. We parted reluc-tantly, but hopeful that by the time he came back for the evening visiting-hour our progeny – son or daughter as maybe – would have arrived. It hadn't, and at the end of a fraught visit he left, almost as depressed as I was at the lack of progress. After a day of listening to the groans and howls of other women – several of whom had arrived after I had, but had given birth and moved on – I found my confidence in a painless childbirth had been replaced by fear of what was still ahead.

It was not until the following afternoon that I was making enough progress to be moved to a side ward, where I was left most of the time alone but with a handbell to ring if I felt the need – and a warning that staff were busy and the bell must not be used lightly. The contractions increased, staff came and went, and between the pain and their visits I listened for the soothing sounds of tugs and boats chugging up and down the Thames outside. As pain and panic combined and enveloped me, I forgot the lessons on how to relax, and when offered gas and air seemed always to be breathing out just when I should have breathed in. Time seemed to stop, or had trapped me in a nightmare in which I was sometimes being torn apart on a medieval rack and at others floating in a mystical state, convinced I was on the brink of understanding the meaning of life.

Around seven o'clock that evening I was at last promoted to the labour ward. Absorbed by then in my own silent, moaning chant – 'Will it never end! Will it never end!' – I heard someone far away say, 'She's working hard.' Later, I sensed rather than saw a flurry of excitement in a room that suddenly seemed full of people, and then I was looking down on the satin-grey creature covered in slime that had slithered to rest against my thigh. 'It's a beautiful boy,' said Sister, who was amongst those who had rushed in to see the birth.

He lay, this changeling, like a stone cherub, a mass of wet hair curled into tendrils over his head, still and quiet. His eyes were closed and he gave no cry before being whisked away. It was an exquisite moment but, exhausted, I too closed my eyes until roused by the blanket of silence that had wrapped itself around me. 'Is something wrong?' I whispered. 'Don't worry,' said Sister. 'Your baby was in a caul, and that's said to be lucky.' So I relaxed and gently drifted into semiconsciousness, unaware that I was experiencing a rare and dangerous complication of childbirth – a post-partum haemorrhage. Emergency action from a hastily called consultant brought me back to consciousness in another brief spell of excruciating pain.

Soon after, Sister was leaning over me and telling me that all was truly well. I asked if I could see my baby, but she said, 'Later. Your husband's here to see you now.' She had a gentle, joyful smile on her face, and her white cap under the lights looked like a saintly halo. It was an effort to smile back, but I did. It was as if there were a close bond between us because of the intensity of the experience we had shared. Still lying on the hard delivery trolley, I turned my head to look at Peter. 'Poor darling,' he said, pushing back a damp strand of hair from my forehead. It hurt him, he told me later, that for him I had no smile.

'Look at him!' cried the nurse as she came towards my bed next day. 'He looks like a schoolboy already!' With his thick crop of light brown hair which she had parted neatly in the centre and brushed flat, with a squashed nose and a large spreading mouth, he looked to me more like a dwarf prize-fighter than a new-born baby. A little alarmed and offended when a medical student came round and said, 'I've seen babies with as much hair before, but never one with such a big mouth', I should perhaps have been prepared for Mum's visit. 'He's not a Noble baby' were her first words. '*All* the Noble babies are beautiful! Still, I expect you think he's lovely. All mothers do.' I felt so exhausted that I did not feel inclined to argue the point, especially as Mum took him from me and held him protectively in her arms.

'Have you made up your mind what you'll call him?' she asked. I told her it was to be Lewis, after an author, Lewis Mumford, Peter and I liked. 'Louis? Lou?' she echoed, disapproval taking her voice up a note or two. 'No! *Lewis* – and he'll be *called* Lewis,' I corrected her, only too aware that she had probably been hoping for a family name – perhaps Alec, George or Walter – and was once again disappointed in the ways of her aberrant daughter. I need not have worried. I had give her the gift of a grandson to dote on and, what is more, one who to her great satisfaction disproved her own prediction. For as time would tell Lewis had inherited in both his looks and his character a pretty large quota of my family's genes.

*

At St Thomas's, some days later, I awoke from an afternoon doze to find the tall, consultant gynaecologist, his hands in the pockets of his white coat, standing at the end of my bed, and a group of medical students around it. It was embarrassing when the consultant, without so much as a greeting, let alone any introduction, began to hold forth as if I were not there. I shut my eyes again and pretended to go on dozing. 'This mother is an example of the miracle of childbirth,' the consultant announced ponderously. I felt a fleeting moment of ridiculous pride before irritation swept it away. That tortuous experience! Some miracle! I thought, and I opened my eyes a fraction to see that one or two of the respectfully silent students had pencils poised to note down the great man's comments. 'This woman has lost enough blood to have left any man in a state of total collapse,' he went on. 'But, as you can see, she has already recovered.' Perhaps it was my rosy cheeks that misled him. I opened my eyes, ready to protest. I wanted to say 'Why don't you ask me how I feel?' But before I could, he had given a curt nod, turned round and swept out – his platoon of misinformed students trailing after him.

14

Homeless Wanderers

Back at Northampton Park the stresses and strains between two young mothers who did not much like each other but had to share stairways and kitchen quickly became intolerable. One day when Mum arrived on a visit she found me wearily filling up a bucket to scrub down the bare wooden stairs because Rita had complained waspishly that I had neglected to do them for weeks. So anaemic that my complexion had by then acquired a shade of almost luminous green, and always tired, I was ready to weep when Mum, let in by Rita, appeared behind me at the top of the attic stairs. She put down her bag, removed her hat, which was a cross between a helmet and a tight posy of dried flowers, rolled up her sleeves and, taking the bucket and scrubbing-brush, said indignantly, 'You're not doing that. Give it here. I'll do it.' Then, in a voice loud enough to be sure it would reach Rita two floors below, she added: 'I should think you've got enough to do looking after the baby at the moment without bothering about these old stairs that look as if they haven't been done for years, never mind weeks.'

A few days later, yet another row broke over me when I was in the kitchen washing nappies – a horrendous job that meant first a lot of rinsing out before I boiled up the nappies in a bucket of water on the gas stove. I was just hiking the steaming bucketful back to the sink when Rita stormed in and ordered me out, there and then. Within three weeks so much unease had built up in the house that it was straining the friendship between Derek and Peter too. When the news of the latest crisis reached Lee, Mum announced: 'Your father says you had all better come over here for a week or two.' As I well knew, calling on Dad's supposed greater authority was a trick Mum had long used to add weight on occasions that she felt it would help get what she wanted. It was not what I wanted, but nor was staying on at Northampton Park.

That weekend we moved into Mum's front room. Peter and I slept on the same old brown rexine bed-settee which I had slept in as an adolescent in the house I had grown up in a few streets away, and which my parents and brothers and cousins had shared with my grandparents until our extended family was broken up by the bombs of the Blitz. It was depressing after all my ambitious dreams to be back again in much the same crowded three-generation household that I had, as I thought, left behind for ever; and worse, to be trapped in the conventional role of housewife and mother I'd somehow meant to escape or at least play differently. Yet it was not all as bad as I had feared. For one thing, with the cooking and most of the washing left to Mum, I had less to do and time to replenish my depleted energy – or, as Mum would have put it, to build up my strength. Best of all, the baby was no longer the unwelcome intruder that he had become at Northampton Park where one of the Ponts' quite reasonable complaints was that whereas their own child slept during the nights like an angel, Lewis seemed to cry through most of them. At Lee he continued creating nightly mayhem for Peter and me, but no one else in the house seemed to mind. For here he was not simply welcomed, but unequivocally absorbed with pride and love as the first of the next generation to join the family.

The brightest spot in the three or four weeks that we remained at Lee was when we heard that Peter had got a new and far more promising job with the Labour Party. Once we could find a home of our own to rent we would, we felt, be through all our difficulties. With the acute housing shortage at the time, the prospect of finding somewhere was not good, and soon after Peter had started at his new job we decided it was time to move on again.

There are some memories – usually painful – that it is easier to forget than to remember, which is probably why I forgot to mention earlier that six weeks before Lewis was born Grace died. We had gone to Great Chesterford to stay for a weekend with Ben while she was in hospital for what we all believed to be a routine operation. Grace was in Addenbrooke's, the teaching hospital in Cambridge, and on the Sunday afternoon we went with Ben to visit her.

As soon as we arrived Grace began to get at Peter. She brushed aside the bunch of flowers he offered her and started her attack. 'However are you going to manage?' she moaned. 'Why have you done this, Peter? It's typical of your selfishness – you never have thought about the consequences of what you do. . . . ' It was hard to take; the more so because it was too soon after her operation to risk answering back. She was agitated already and her face was flushed. 'There's no need to worry about us, Grace,' I said sympathetically, hoping to soothe things over. 'We are fine. *I* am not worried, so why should you be?'

Peter said nothing. He knew her consuming sense of grievance too well, and that it was not just about him but about life having treated her less well than she believed it ought to have done. Even so, he was hurt (who wouldn't have been?) at this latest attack on his general irresponsibility, which had now become a failure to love and care for me. In the back of the Hillman, Peter sat beside me hunched up and subdued as Ben drove us home to Rose Cottage. Unable to speak freely to each other about what had happened, we held hands tightly and listened to Ben, who chatted on with determined cheerfulness about Grace's recovery and how soon he might expect her to be discharged.

Back in the cottage, we were ready to pour out the tea I had made on our arrival when the telephone rang. Ben picked up the receiver. It was the hospital asking him to return at once. When he got there he was told that, almost immediately after we left the hospital, Grace had unexpectedly died. Across the lane from the cottage lived a young Australian doctor who worked at Addenbrooke's. Dr Andrew Holland and his wife had become friends of Ben and Grace and, before Ben returned, the news had reached them. When they heard Ben's car returning up the lane they came across and followed him in.

Ben's round, pink face was wet with tears, almost as if his grief was oozing out through his skin, but in his gentlemanly way he assured Andrew that although he appreciated his kindness there was for the moment nothing he could do. I don't think Ben expected either Peter or me to share his deep grief, and indeed he seemed specially concerned, because of the advanced stage of my pregnancy, that I should not be upset. Whether or not Ben remembered Grace's last unhappy outburst, I knew from the dismayed expression when he looked at his father mopping his face and moustache with his already damp handkerchief that Peter did.

Barely taking the time to take off his coat Ben began to bustle about making lists, looking up telephone numbers and sorting through the drawers of his desk for papers he said he would need. Or perhaps it was that he wanted to find, for one of the things he brought out was a letter he had received from Grace, which he pressed into my hands and begged me to read. This woman who had so often seemed to agitate Ben almost beyond endurance with her constant whining and bickering – about his slowness in cleaning the silver, the miserable pension he would get when he retired, the shame of the outside lavatory – had written to him from the hospital only two days earlier. In her letter there were no complaints, no nagging reminders to bring along her soap or a clean towel or her powder-puff. Hers was a passionate cry from the heart in which she poured out her need and her longing for him. 'She loved you very much, Ben,' I said to console him, at the same time amazed and bemused that what I was saying must actually be true.

Sad and lonely as he was, and hearing of our difficulties after Lewis's arrival, Ben was quick to offer us a home with him for the time being (as we saw it) and – for him – in the hope that it might become permanent. We knew it would mean a long day for Peter commuting to London and back, perhaps loneliness for me, but anything was better than going back to Northampton Park. Pleased to get rid of us, Derek and Rita said that we could leave our bits of furniture behind; and so off we went again in early November to join Ben at Rose Cottage for an indefinite stay.

Neither my nostalgic childhood memories of country holidays in the Bedfordshire village from which my mother had come, nor my happy days as a WAAF on a remote airfield in Norfolk during the war turned out to be much of a preparation for the long, dark, winter days of the daily routine which I now found myself locked into in rural Essex. Once both Peter and Ben had left for the day, I found that tidying round, doing the nappies and tending to the wakeful Lewis took up most of the morning, but the rest of the day often dragged. 'I still find it very lonely here,' I wrote to my friend Meg in January. 'Sometimes I feel awfully sorry for myself as I mooch down lonely country roads pushing a ruminating baby. Yesterday was a bad day – tears were streaming down my face with self-pity as I wandered along. It seems in my lowest moods that I'm being punished and pushed out of my world because I've had a baby.'

It was not that the inhabitants of the village were unfriendly; it was that I was not willing to adjust to a very different way of life. One day, for example, when I arrived home from a walk, I was told by Ben's domestic helper (who came in once a week) that Miss Penhurst had called and left her card. I was incredulous: could it be that after the upheavals of five years of war this kind of formal 'social call' still existed? I did not return the call, but some weeks later Miss Penhurst returned. She was a beanpole of a woman, dressed in a narrow grey coat and a brown bucket-shaped hat that looked as if they belonged to the 1920s rather than the brink of the 1950s. I soon realized that I was being not so much visited as vetted – to find out where in the social hierarchy of the village I was to be fitted. Out of consideration for Ben (and the memory of Grace) I offered tea, but was relieved when this was refused. By the time Miss Penhurst left I had made it perfectly clear that I had no intention of joining in the church activities she had suggested might interest me and that, unlike my father-in-law, I did not share her (Conservative) political beliefs.

Another character in the village, although very different from Miss Penhurst, was Percy Hill. Small, hunch-shouldered and rather deaf, Percy Hill and his wife Eva, a wispy-haired, quiet and gentle woman, lived in a tall, timbered and thatched house set in spacious grounds along a lane leading off the centre of the village. I don't know how long Percy had lived in Great Chesterford, but it was long enough for him to have bought up large parts of it and also of its near-neighbour, Little Chesterford. He was a wealthy man and an extremely cocky (and Cockney) one who never tired of proclaiming his self-made success.

Percy owned not only a substantial part of Great Chesterford but of other property in Bloomsbury, where he had at some stage lived, had built up a successful building and property business and reputedly been on more than one occasion mayor of the old borough of Holborn. He had two unmarried daughters – with old-fashioned names like Gert and Daisy – who during the week lived in one of the Bloomsbury flats owned by their father. Although they were well into their thirties (if not forties), Percy expected them to come at weekends to be indulged or bullied by him, according to his mood.

Improbably, as it seemed to Peter and me, this brash little man had become a friend of Ben and Grace, both of whom cruelly mocked his rough manners in private but never refused an invitation to his house. To be fair, Ben and Grace were very fond of Percy's cowed wife Eva. It was a mystery how and why such a gentle, gracious and well-bred woman as Eva should have come to marry a man whose main aim seemed to be to humiliate her. She herself was a charming hostess, always smiling sweetly and as caring about her guests as she seemed, despite his neglect, to be about Percy, one of whose favourite tricks was to force conversation round to some story about his first wife that invariably ended up with the phrase 'My first wife – she was an angel.'

Another of the mysteries about Percy Hill was that his brashness was not at all reflected in his surroundings. He was a collector, and his home was a veritable museum of beautiful antiques. Of course they were also valuable, and Percy delighted in telling how little he had paid for this marvel or that; or how he had realized long before others that these enamel-topped boxes were worth collecting and so he had paid practically nothing for them. Although the beautiful garden was largely the fruition of Eva's care and knowledge of plants, Percy was in charge of the orchard and its harvest. One of the few occasions I really enjoyed talking to him was when he invited me to look round the large outhouse in which his fruit harvest was stored. The smell of the apples lying spaced out along slatted shelves perhaps sweetened my perception, but as we walked round – with Percy explaining the qualities of each variety and stopping to examine and throw out any fruit that showed mould or bruising – he was no longer the vainglorious braggart but a happy, contented countryman.

At the bottom end of the village's social scale were the Sharpe sisters, who were amusing to talk to when I called on them once a week to buy eggs, but whose interests were almost entirely restricted to those of the village and its inhabitants, and hardly at all to those that I rated so highly – such as problems of social welfare. The Sharpes lived in another large, very old cottage opposite the bottom of Rose Lane, where their chickens scratched about in the dusty, weed-strewn yard that surrounded the house. They were regarded as decidedly odd by most of the villagers, and as peasants by the élite such as Miss Penhurst.

The 'Sharpe ladies', as Ben liked to call them with jocular irony, seemed to be very poor, although the elder Miss Sharpe must have earned something because it was she who delivered the post to the outlying farms and cottages, riding round on her old upright and heavy black bicycle. Their clothes always looked ragged and their nails were black with impacted grime. The only water they had came from a tap in the yard, and inside the house dirt-ingrained lace curtains allowed little light through. But there was enough to catch the gleam of fine old china and beautiful glassware that stood on the window-sill, mantelpiece and dresser and had, they said, come down to them from their parents, like the house. To talk to the Sharpes was to walk into a time-warp. They loved to gossip, usually with sly darts of spiteful humour aimed at their fellow-villagers. They had lived all their lives in the village and regarded London – fifty miles away – as a distant planet they liked to hear stories about but had no desire to visit. If I had been looking more with the eyes of a novelist than social worker, I should have seen that the Sharpes were worth far more attention than I gave them. Even then, despite my blinkered perception, they were remarkable enough for me to wonder whether in an earlier age they might have been seen not just as odd characters but as witches.

As winter set in and the days became shorter and darker, my days at Rose Cottage seemed even longer and lonelier – days that began with a frosty early morning walk to the station to see Peter off on the train to London, and which by lunchtime had the washing frozen hard on the line in the garden.

In January we migrated again to Lee for a month because of the extra long working hours that the forthcoming General Election would mean for Peter, in his new job. After four weeks in London during which our hopes were first raised, then dashed, of finding a place to rent, it was back again to Great Chesterford, where Ben told us apologetically that an old family friend, known to Peter in his childhood as Aunt Jess, wanted to come and stay. Always soft-hearted, Ben explained that he could not refuse her because she was temporarily without a home. I faced her arrival with mixed feelings.

14 March
This winter seems endless. Each day I think I can't go on any longer. Yet each day I'm still here to smile at Peter on his return! Now Jess is here. There's no doubt that she is a character, but to stay here long with her here too in this tiny cottage! Still, so far it's been interesting to hear from her of Peter's early days. To learn what a quaint child he was – 'either a genius or a comedian'. Good to learn too how much Dorrie, his mother, loved him and how she worried at having to leave him, and of his sad little comment after she died 'Was my Mummy very unkind? She didn't ask me to her funeral.'

Jess's background was mysterious. She was small, with a flat nose and slanting eyes, and hair that was still jet-black. It was clear that she was at least partly Oriental, but Ben had warned me before she arrived: 'She doesn't like anyone to talk about that.' (It provoked an infuriated comment from me to Peter when he got home that evening: 'Does he think I'm going to say to her when she arrives, "Hallo, Chinkee?"!') Whatever her origins, Jess had private means and, as well as having been a present-giving 'aunt' to Peter, and Grace's two daughters, she had also been a quite generous benefactor to Ben and Grace in the past. She had never married, and for some years had chosen to live as a paying quest in lodgings, from which she moved whenever she became dissatisfied with the services she received.

I soon found that Jess intended to contribute no more to the practical running of the household than she had as a paying guest in lodgings. Worse, that she meant to impose her wishes on all of us so that her rigid daily routines were not disrupted. Ben (who had to turn out of the smaller second bedroom to sleep on a divan squeezed under the eaves on the landing at the top of the stairs) accepted without demur that he should wake Jess with morning tea, take her hot water for washing, and empty her chamber-pot before he left for work. I was less willing to be pressed into starting to get lunch ready before I had settled Lewis for his morning nap, and boiled up and hung out his nappies. Impatient as Jess was for her lunch at 11.30 a.m., then ready for afternoon tea at 2.30 p.m. and supper at 5 p.m., her hurry to get through the day at least had the advantage that she went off to bed before 9 p.m., which left some of the evening for us to enjoy without her. For the awful thing was that Jess proved to be as determined to bicker and complain with and about Ben as Grace had been.

As the long days with Jess continued I began to realize that I was being drawn into the quarrels and passions of a distant past, but one that to Jess was far more vivid and important than the present. It emerged that the feelings she held for both Grace and Ben were as much about jealousy and hate as about love, and dominated by the tragic figure of Peter's mother. As day after day I was bombarded by Jess's accusations of the wicked reprobate, Ben, and the seductive Grace 'carrying on' even as 'poor Dorrie' lay dying, I found out what it was to be brainwashed. For every day it was a shock when, with the cheery 'Hallo, my dears' that invariably announced his arrival, it wasn't the demon portrayed by Jess who burst in through the front door, but the familiar, kindly figure of my father-in-law. Some weeks later, to my relief, Jess left. She had found herself new lodgings in a neighbouring village, near enough to ensure that Ben would visit her. It was then that I began to wonder if, all those years ago, in the 1920s, she herself had hoped to replace Dorrie in Ben's affections, and that it was her disappointment at not having done so that she could not forget.

15
Ups and Downs

It was while I was still at work at Hackney Hospital that Peter had followed up the note he had seen in *The Observer* about a new pamphlet with the evocative title of *Small Man, Big World*. Peter got hold of a copy, read it, knew that he was at one with the thoughts expressed in it and wrote to the author, Michael Young, asking to meet him. A reply came suggesting a lunchtime meeting in a pub conveniently close to the Labour Party's headquarters where Michael was the head of the research department. By the time they met, Peter had left Ruskin College and was back in London and the birth of our baby was imminent. The meeting went well and before they parted Peter asked whether there might be any jobs coming up in the research department. To his disappointment there were not, and so it was back to the boring work as a temporary clerk.

A few weeks later, and only just after I had returned with Lewis to Northampton Park, where tensions were building up rapidly, the exciting news came that an unexpected vacancy at the Labour Party as a research assistant had come up, for which Peter could apply. The main task would be to write a fortnightly pamphlet called *Talking Points*, which aimed to give useful ammunition on current issues to active Party workers, and also Members of Parliament. Unusually, the normal procedure of advertising the post was not to be followed because someone was needed who could take the job over immediately. It was therefore proposed that candidates should compete for the job by doing a sample *Talking Points*.

Up in our attic rooms, Peter sat down at the little satinwood desk and tried to get to work on his draft. It was not easy with the baby crying most of the time in the next room and me increasingly agitated because I had no idea why. Was he crying because he had indigestion from getting too much milk from my overflowing breasts? Or was he getting too little, even though the health visitor's advice was that with such a plentiful supply 'two minutes each side' was all he needed? Despite her assurance that all mothers soon learn to know what different cries mean when their babies cry, this did not seem to apply to me. And much as he wanted to help, Peter could hardly be expected to be any wiser. On top of this, there were the nights of broken sleep, as well as the atmosphere of ill-will hanging like a pall over the household.

It was hardly surprising that when he came home to all this at the end of the daily grind in his second temporary job at the St Pancras Electricity Company (where the work although slightly better paid was as boring as the first one) Peter found it difficult to concentrate on writing a 'dummy draft' of *Talking Points*. Indeed, he was so discouraged that he came to the conclusion that in the limited time before it had to be sent in he simply could not do it. I knew very well the difficulties and disappointments Peter was experiencing and, convinced by this time that I was a good part of the cause of them, I did not feel I could press him too hard to go on. This was not the line that Michael Young took when Peter telephoned to say that he had decided to withdraw. 'I think that would be a mistake,' Michael Young told him. 'I think you stand a very good chance.'

By the time we heard that Peter had got the job we had decamped from Northampton Park for our respite stay at Lee where, of course, everyone was as pleased and excited as we were at this change in our fortunes. To them, as much as to us, it seemed like riches, this sudden jump from the weekly wage of £6 paid by the St Pancras Electricity Company (which had been £1 a week more than he earned at the Income Tax Office) to the princely annual salary of £495 the new job offered. But for Peter and me it was not merely the better money that was so exciting; it was the prospect of work of interest and value, of knowing that if all went well during his probationary six months Peter would be really on the way to a career of a kind we both believed to be worthwhile.

I had known, of course, that both the Income Tax Office

and the Electricity Company jobs had been boring for Peter.
But it was only after they were over that he was willing to
admit just how disappointed and trapped he had felt going
off, day after day, to perform the same checking or clerical
function over and over again. It was only now that it was
behind us that he could tell me how he had hated this even
more than he had being an apprentice in the car factory and
almost as much as being in the mines.

Peter started work at Transport House in Smith Square –
where the Labour Party then had its headquarters – in early
September. After discussion with his senior, Wilfred, and on
specially important issues with Michael as well, Peter was to
write each issue of *Talking Points* and get it to the printers.
When the proofs were ready he went to the Odhams Press
building, which was in Covent Garden, to check, cut or ex-
pand as necessary.

By 1949, bedevilled with economic crises and world shortages, the Labour Government was finding it difficult to keep its
promises of a better life for all in post-war Britain. Only two
weeks later, on 18 September (coinciding with Peter's twenty-
sixth birthday), devaluation was the latest shock that had to be
explained to the appalled Party activists for whom he was writing. Within a few months of his arrival, he was pitched into
other work such as writing *Speakers' Notes* for the 1950 General
Election, or editing *Campaign Notes* which, during the election
(and the subsequent election in 1951), were posted out to local
parties the morning after they were written. In those pre-Fax
days, it meant Peter had to drive out to Odhams print works
at Watford in a hired car each night to check the proofs.
Later, working with ministers and other political figures in
the Party, acting as secretary to committees, tutoring at summer
schools, talking to local Labour Party groups and attending
Party conferences were all to become part of the job.

It was for the month leading up to the March 1950 election, knowing as we did that Peter would have to be working particularly hard, that we moved back to my parents'
home again. It meant his journeys to work and back would
take less than a third of the time it took him to get to Great
Chesterford and back. South-east London had a new attraction for me too, for at least in London there were plenty of

shops at the end of the road where shopkeepers like Mr Baxter at the Co-op butchers who had known me since childhood were ready to greet me warmly. And I could dawdle through the park where the public library in the old manor house of Lee was always a place in which I could enjoy a leisurely browse. Even at home with Mum there was more going on, what with telephone calls and Dad or his workmen coming and going in the yard beside the house. It helped too – although it meant sharing Peter with the family when he returned from central London – that in spite of having to work later most days he usually got back early enough to join in bathing Lewis and getting him to bed.

It was not like having the place of our own we longed for, but I was grateful that Mum and Dad were prepared to put themselves out so much to help us. Although Mum never complained, I knew that, to her, giving up her prized front room was no small sacrifice – far more so than the extra burden of feeding and cooking which our visits entailed. Apart from a bit of shopping, motherhood had not much improved my skill as a housewife and I continued to do little other than look after my son. Far from resenting this, Mum seemed relieved to find that I was capable of caring for Lewis as well as I did, although she was never slow to voice her opinion on my lack of skill. 'Give him to me. You just don't seem to know how to hold him,' she said one day, with that hint of superiority which in earlier years would have infuriated me but now made me smile. For I knew that she was justified. Just as she could get the nappies done, hanging out and miraculously white in half the time I took, so could she get Lewis to relax into contented chuckles within minutes.

Looking across at her as she sat on the other side of the fire-place with Lewis, sprawled out on her capacious lap one after-noon, I knew that because of him the bonds of affection between us had been strengthened. Perhaps for my mother it was partly that, however unwillingly on my side, I was now joined with her in what she felt to be women's inevitable lot. But for both of us, and far more important, was our shared love of this child who by now Mum had rocked into slumber. Raising her eyebrows, and putting a warning finger to her lips, she care-fully stood up and carried Lewis into the front room to put him in his pram. When she came back, she stood looking in the mirror above the fireplace, titivating her tobacco-brown hair. Yes, you're quite right, I thought. You still look quite good for a fifty-eight-year-old. Satisfied with her image, she turned to me with her brown eyes shining and said, 'Well, how about a cup of tea now we've got a bit of peace and quiet?' I knew that at the day's end, in the privacy of their bedroom upstairs, she would quite likely be grumbling mildly to Dad about all the extra chores our latest invasion was putting on her. But when I said, 'I'll make the tea', she promptly replied, 'No. It's too much like hot water when you do it. Read your book for a moment.' It was not so surprising, I thought, having a mother like mine, that I should be so ambivalent about being put into the same mould. She had never concealed her recurrent resentment of her role as wife and mother, yet at the same time she got so much satisfaction from it.

What was more of a mystery was why 'the boys' (my two brothers and two cousins), after all their journeying to exotic parts, were so different. There was no ambivalence for them. Only too happy to return to Lee, they had already settled back into much the same style of life they had led before being called up for war service. Wal had not only been glad to get back to Lee, but even before the war began had decided to give up commuting to the City to do office work and to throw in his lot with Dad in the building trade. Cousin Pete, who had ended his time in the Army as a captain and had therefore been picked out for higher things when he returned to his firm, loathed rather than welcomed the idea that this would before long mean his having to move to some other part of the country. As for Joe and Ken, both had returned happily to the same sorts of jobs they had been trained to do before the war. And although all four were to do well in their future careers, they were content to go on sharing the parental home until marriage beckoned.

By the time we returned to Great Chesterford after the election, as Jess was no longer there and Lewis was growing and thriving, living in the country seemed in some ways slightly less bleak and dreary:

Tuesday, 21 March 1950

A good spring day. Nothing seems quite so bad in such weather. Lewis is beside me, with fluffy hair, rosy cheeks, sparkling violet-blue eyes, and hanging on to the side of his playpen with outrageous delight and self-satisfaction. He 'da-da's' or grunts happily, or silently munches his gums together. It seems impossible, and yet it's surely true, each day he becomes more beautiful.

I had discovered that, along with its burdens, motherhood had its joys and satisfactions; but for me, far more than my mother, this was not enough. Each day by the time Peter returned I was thirsting for news of *his* day at work, and although this was a source of absorbing interest to both of us it often enhanced more than alleviated my feeling of being an exile from life.

'Walking to the station to see Peter off this morning I realized the hedges are *just* green again. The brown of winter is gone. This of course is a delight, but I'm so tired of my life here in such a weary, weary way. This year, I shall not find spring singing through me with upsurging hopes. Although each day I am *expectant* for I know not what, each day I am worn out by waiting – for Peter, for the future, for life to begin again.'

16

A Slum in Hackney

As Peter got to know his colleagues at the Labour Party I formed the impression from my distant and no doubt distorted view that the Welsh were strongly represented there. And this was not only because Aneurin Bevan's star was so evidently rising (wartime maverick, then Minister of Health, and Labour's most powerful orator inside and outside Parliament), but because the General Secretary of the Party in 1950 was the Welsh Morgan Phillips and his chief assistant another Welshman called Gwilym Williams. Just after the 1950 General Election, and a few weeks after we had returned to Great Chesterford, Peter came home with the exciting news that Gwilym was planning to move and thought that it might be possible for us to take over his present tenancy if we wanted it. Gwilym warned Peter that this was no palace, merely 'a slum in Hackney' that might do for us until something better came along – as it now had for him and his wife.

From then on we waited impatiently for this dream to become reality. We had already had too many disappointments. Dad's contacts in Lee had thrown up one or two possibilities, and although the last thing I wanted to do was to settle down permanently in the district where I had grown up, I was disappointed when these fell through. Once Peter had been appointed to the permanent staff at the Labour Party, in our desperation we even began to consider taking out a mortgage to buy a property. It would not be easy, for we had no capital – and indeed by this time no savings at all – and buying would be possible only if we could find something at a very low price. By good luck, we did. It was a late Georgian house in a small area of terraced streets perched on the hillside very close to Greenwich Park and the northern edge of Blackheath.

As soon as we saw it I knew that this was a home I could be happy in. We found that the rooms were small, with two on each of three floors. There was also a basement floor in which one room opened on to a small yard at ground level at the back of the house, with a second entirely below ground which had been turned into a rudimentary bathroom. It was a pretty house, but what was far more than pretty were the views it had from the back windows and the garden. Below, as the hill fell away, were the roof-tops of Deptford, with glimpses of the silvery curves of the Thames beyond and, in the distance, a sweeping panorama of central London dominated by the dome of St Paul's. The price of this little gem was £750.

Dad had offered to look over it with his skilled builder's eye to see what work would be needed to make it habitable. He went over on his own one Sunday morning to look at it. In his opinion it was basically sound, but because the house opened straight on to the street (and he had found people in the terrace sitting outside on kitchen chairs!), he thought it was overpriced. Although Peter and I considered this simply reflected his view of a suburban respectability that we did not share, we took his advice about price and offered £600. We were overjoyed when this was accepted, but again Dad's reaction was not ours. Eager to get the best bargain he could for us, and suspicious because the offer had been accepted so promptly and without the kind of bargaining he enjoyed, he pressed us to make a yet lower bid – this time of £475. A fortnight later when we had had no reply Peter got in touch with the estate agent to find out why there had been no response to our offer. He was told coldly it was no longer available. (We were so discouraged by this experience that it was fifteen years before we entered the house-buying market!)

No further offers came our way until, two months later, the prospect of the 'slum in Hackney' turned up, and by early autumn we moved to the top two floors of a plain, yellow-brick Victorian house hemmed in on three sides by streets, the one at the front of the house being the main road between Dalston Junction and Mare Street. We had two rooms and a kitchen on the first floor, and one large room on the floor above that had been divided into two by a light partition. The back room on the top floor was not ours, and was crammed with broken-down furniture belonging to the landlord. It had been left there from the time he or his parents had moved out to some outlying suburb from what had been the family home. The landlord insisted he had to keep the back room so that he had the right to regain possession of the house if ever he wanted to, unlikely as that seemed to be to us. We christened it 'the junk-room' – and felt free from time to time to add bits of our own to the general mess.

The stairs were meagrely covered with well-worn lino; kitchen, bedroom and hall were painted in nondescript shades of beige, and in our sitting-room there was a depressing patterned wallpaper of pink and brown ferns. The landlord was proud of these decorative features and made it clear that he would not permit any changes to them. As he came in person to collect the monthly rent, there was little we could do but put up with all of this, and we had to forgo the modern, slightly arty surroundings that I had hoped to achieve. We had the use of the bath in the kitchen of the ground-floor tenants (two young women who were employed in a nearby day nursery). We seldom exercised this right because it was too much trouble to fix a convenient time (and I was afraid of the explosive noises made by the very old geyser). We had to make do with hot water from a gas heater that the landlord allowed us to install over the kitchen sink – at our own expense. There was one shared lavatory on the ground floor, and shared use of the neglected patch of ground that could hardly be called a back garden but could be used to hang out the washing by tenants (including the young married couple who lived in the enviably self-contained semi-basement flat).

With our minimal furnishings retrieved from the Ponts' attic rooms, we were content to make what we could of our first proper home. Dad found us a small, rexine-covered sofa, which I covered up as well as I could with another find of his – what I took to be an old cotton bedspread. It was a nicely woven material in stripes of navy blue and maroon which, years later, long after I had thrown it out, I realized Dad had been quite right to say was 'not rubbish'. It was a Turkish kelim. We partly covered the floor with coconut matting, which proved to be a great collector of dust and was hard to clean even after we bought the reconditioned vacuum cleaner a door-to-door salesman later persuaded us to buy. Our prized green and gold curtains went up again in the window, and made a pleasant frame to the twirling, silver-green foliage of the grey poplar tree which was the one lovely feature in the garden patch below.

A cot for Lewis, some old curtains of Mum's, and a chair went into the smaller part of the partitioned bedroom. For our part I bought yards of the cheapest cotton dress material I could find to make curtains and a cover for a low double divan (another junk-shop bargain that Peter had picked up while at Ruskin College). The cotton material was black but so thin that it was almost diaphanous, and it had an overall pattern of tiny white daisies. While Mum thought it a very strange choice, I loved it. In the daytime, although the bare floor-boards were stained black, with the plain walls the room looked surprisingly charming; and at nights, when the bright lights from the street-lamps outside shone through the thin material, the room was suffused with a luminous silvery glow that transformed it. We needed this bit of magic on nights when Lewis woke us with his cries, which although by now a walking and talking toddler he still did on most nights.

The black curtains turned out to have another advantage, and this was that they did not need frequent washing. The combination of the dust thrown up from the traffic and the street, the coal-fires – which were then most people's only form of heating, including ours – and the dirt that oozed from the crevices in walls and floor-boards made cleaning a constant battle. Coal-fires also meant soot, and when the sweep came to clean the chimney, even though he brought the new-style industrial vacuum cleaner, a film of soot afterwards settled on everything. I learnt the hard way that omitting to get the sweep in could be even worse, when one day the chimney caught fire, the flames roaring with terrifying fury. Great clods of compacted soot dropped into the grate and broke up and spilled out of the grate on to the coconut matting, followed by a mountain of red-hot ash. Soon I could feel waves of heat coming out of the brickwork of the chimney-breast. I knew I ought to call the fire brigade (if a neighbour had not done so already on seeing the black smoke belching out on the roof), but by the time I had made up my mind that I must pick up Lewis and run to find a telephone the blaze had died down.

Apart from council housing and one or two old blocks built by philanthropic charitable trusts that were purpose built and self-contained, most of the old Victorian housing in our part of Hackney in the 1950s was in multi-occupation and in varying states of crumbling decline. There were few owner-occupiers, and hardly any middle-class professionals (as the health visitor, eager to help me find young mothers with whom I would have something in common, pointed out to me). The homes hidden behind spotless white net curtains in the streets round about seemed to be those of respectable, independent-minded people, including skilled, semi-skilled and clerical workers, most of whom had lived in the district for years and were intent on keeping 'themselves to themselves'.

It was rare to see any non-white person in the Hackney neighbourhood. Many months after our arrival there I got on a bus at the stop close to the house to go shopping with Lewis in Kingsland Road and was surprised to see that the conductor was black. He would have been one of the advance guard of the West Indians who were soon to be encouraged in large numbers to come to Britain to ease the acute labour shortage in London Transport and the hospitals. Lewis stared at the man, and to my consternation continued to do so every time he walked past us to collect more fares. When I saw he was about to say something, I leant over him, hoping to focus his attention firmly on me. 'Mummy,' he piped up in that high-pitched voice of the young child which carries only too well, 'hasn't that man got a *lovely* red tongue.' For the first time – but not the last – this comment brought home to me that until they are taught otherwise, skin colour is unremarkable to the very young.

A hundred yards along the road from us was the office of the local Labour Party, with which we soon became actively involved. Though there were neither blacks nor professional class people who belonged to it, the Party included a few Jewish members and many other keen and active local people of both sexes and all ages. Young Bob Masters, for example, who had been elected to the borough council at the age of twenty-one, and came from a keenly political extended family who lived only a couple of streets away. I got to know his sister, Peggy, and whenever I called in at their home the kettle was always 'just on the boil' and tea about to be made.

Living in a gloomy, but self-contained, flat in Victorian

buildings of red brick at the other end of the road were the Bassets, a retired couple who still spoke with a hint of the East Anglian accent of their childhood. Mrs Basset, plump, rosy-faced and kindly, was proud of the careful housekeeping that her husband's regular, but meagre, earnings on the railways had always made necessary. Long married, they were a happily contented pair and, when I called in one day, Mr Basset nodded in approving confirmation as his wife explained how many meals she could get from a pound of sausages. Like all but the very comfortably off she had no refrigerator, but she had found that if she boiled them first, and then kept them in her cool larder, she could fry them up later, as needed, and so make them last most of the week.

Far more assiduous at attending meetings than I was (for someone had to be at home in the evenings to look after Lewis), Peter, when he became ward secretary, made a good friend of the middle-aged Jewish man who was Party chairman and a revered figure on the local council. Abe was a self-educated intellectual. A Communist in belief, but far too humane to be more than moderately Socialist in practice, he became for a while almost a father-figure to Peter. Devoted to the cause as well as to Hackney and its people, Abe – for the sake of his growing family – decided reluctantly to move out into one of the new suburban estates in Essex as more and more other families were about to do.

Although I attended important ward meetings, such as elections of ward Party representatives to management committees, I found that the long-winded pontificating in which the men mostly indulged (and seemed so to enjoy) were not my idea of fun. I found the women's group meetings easier (and sometimes enjoyable), probably because the subjects chosen for discussion were usually both more practical and more relevant to women's interests. I think the only significant contribution I ever made was to press for a resolution to remove lead paint from children's toys. It was passed unanimously at the meeting, and sent on its way to be discussed and agreed, as we in the women's group happily believed, at the next Labour Party conference. Somewhere on the way it got lost – as I ruefully noted when I read more than thirty-five years later that legislation to ban lead paint in children's toys had just been passed.

As I got to know the neighbourhood through passing

conversations with young mothers or old people on my daily walks with Lewis to nearby London Fields or the local shops, I became aware how different their experience, and indeed mine, was from how things were according to the propaganda I read in the *Talking Points* Peter proudly brought home for me to see. Though under the daily stresses of motherhood I found it harder to find time to note down my thoughts, this was one occasion when I did:

It's all very well for Peter to tell me that the cost of living since last June has only gone up three points, but it just doesn't seem to bear any relation to the facts in the shops. Of course, there is something in what he says – that it is easier to notice when things go up than when they stay the same or go down. In fact that is one of the troubles, everyone seems so keen to believe the worst. I'm sure I don't imagine that the girls in the Co-op get quite a kick out of telling me that *this* has gone up this much, and *this* and *that*. It isn't that they mean to be propagandists for the Tories, but more that it's a means of being friendly and having a nice shared grumble.

Another place you get the same thing is in the queues. I sometimes wonder whether *any* socialists apart from me are registered at our Co-op. 'It's near starvation – no other country in the world puts up with what we do. All the rest have all the meat they want', I heard someone moaning the other day. And the dreadful thing is that no one took the woman up on what she said. Certainly I didn't. Everyone gave non-committal sighs and grunts. Of course, I should speak up. But why don't I? One reason is because the housewife bit of me finds it hard to defend. I mean [a weekly ration of], 8d [pence] worth of meat! What housewife who has to queue for this can believe she and her other housewives have not got a grievance.

Things did not change much after the General Election of 1950 when the Labour Government was replaced by a Conservative one, but from then on *Talking Points* no longer had to defend Labour's policies. Austerity (and rationing) continued to make life difficult, but now it was 'them' – the Conservatives – who were doing badly on housing or the economy, not 'us'. Even on our 'princely salary' it seemed increasingly hard to manage so that, as on one occasion I bitterly remarked to Peter, just a new yellow duster (costing sixpence in Woolworth's) was an unaffordable luxury.

Poverty and love are bad companions, as Mum had so often and so bitterly impressed on me in the hard interwar years during which I grew up. Now I found that when marital quarrels broke out between me and Peter it was most often about money, or the lack of it. A quarrel that started over some modest or imagined extravagance of Peter's would stir up my feelings of being trapped in the same way as Mum had been (and that I had been so cockily sure I would never be). When I rejected, as he saw it, his reasoned response, and always distressed by my anger, Peter would offer any olive branch he could find to mollify me. 'I know you want a fight,' he said dejectedly in response to one of my stormy attacks, 'but I just can't do it.' Often his attempts at peace-making merely increased my fury or, worse still, launched me into a sulk that could linger for days, poisoning the atmosphere and sometimes tipping me into further self-punishing depression that was even harder to get out of.

It was not until long after we had left Hackney that Peter risked trying to match my verbal aggressiveness with some of his own. Astonished when he did, I collapsed into laughter. 'That's not fair!' I exclaimed. 'You are hitting back!' It took longer still before I was secure enough *almost* to give up my devastating sulks.

17

Old Friends and New

Dirty, noisy, with its crumbling housing, few open green spaces and not very accessible, Hackney had little to attract those without good reason to come to it. As my friend Daphne, excusing herself for not having visited earlier, bluntly pointed out, 'I'm afraid when one's free time is limited, one does tend to put first friends who live in nice places.' I could see what she meant, remembering the occasion soon after we had moved in when another former colleague from Hackney Hospital – the overgrown Girl Guider – decided to call in on me unasked. Having offered her a cup of tea and gone to the kitchen to make it, I found as I brought it into the sitting-room that she was in the process of rubbing her fingers along the crossbar of the sash window. 'Look at this!' she said, holding out a dirty hand. 'This isn't good enough! But I suppose keeping clean in this sort of place must be a *nightmare*.' At least, I thought, as I saw her out, she's not likely to call again. She didn't.

Such discouraging reactions did not stop us from turning our second living-room into a spare room for the friends we hoped might come not just to pop in but to stay. We put another bit of coconut matting on the floor, at the window more of Mum's old curtains (happening to be in a favourite colour of here, rose pink, they went quite well with the improbable roses of the wallpaper), and one of the single beds we no longer needed. I think the only friend who came to stay was Meg, but happily she came so often that before long the room became known to all of us as 'Meg's room'.

Meg had successfully completed her social science diploma at Bedford College and was determined to fulfil the dream of living abroad, which we had so eagerly shared soon after we met as teenagers. Shut up as we had been in 'fortress Britain' during the war, it had been an impossible dream for us then. Now for Meg, still single and free, it was at last about to become reality. As soon as her final term at university had ended, she set off for Norway, where she planned to stay all summer. Stranded in Canonbury in the last stages of my pregnancy, I waited impatiently for letters that might give me at least a taste of the exciting time I was sure she must be having. None came, and she did not get back until after Lewis was born. By then I was so eager to see her that, on the day she was coming, I waited outside for her, wheeling Lewis up and down the street in his pram. She told me in later years that, as she turned the corner and caught sight of me, she knew it was a picture she would never forget. It was not that I was slim again, or that my dark hair was fluffed out instead of in its familiar sleek page-boy style; not even the stylishly fashionable new dress with its long full skirt and fitted waist that I was wearing. It was the contrast between my elegance and the tattiness of the worn green pram I was trundling along with such apparent pride.

I think that my sense of pride was in Lewis more than my new look, and partly to boost my own flagging morale – as well as my need to conceal the envy I felt of Meg in her recent adventure. Yet, although none of this was ever expressed openly between us, I suspect that at the same time in some ways Meg envied me. As long as I had known her it had always been clear that she had little, if any, of the ambivalence that I had about marriage and motherhood. She saw both as natural and necessary parts of a happy future that she was becoming increasingly impatient to reach. However, as she and Jake had sensibly decided that for them marriage must wait until he had finished his studies at Oxford, she now had to find a job and, what is more, be content (as I had found I could not be) to be apart from Jake except for occasional weekends in term-time and during the vacations.

While Jake was away Meg would come often to supper and stay for the night. In vacations Jake would also turn up to enliven our evenings with his outrageous but always witty opinions. More often pacing about the room than sitting down, and with his auburn hair shining in the light and the glitter of his amber-coloured eyes enhanced by the draught cider that he and Peter had gone to the local pub to bring back in a jug, he always offered some spark to start things off. On one occasion he complained wittily of one political figure he had taken against: 'He's gone woody in the middle, like an old pear.' On another evening a recent discussion in the House of Lords on euthanasia was the focus of his indignation. 'Oh, how they love their principles!' he exploded. 'With what vigour they rush to protect the community from the menace of wicked doctors! "Slippery slopes", "value of human life", "where would it end?", "look at Germany" – cliché after cliché they drop like dumplings.' Religion, politics, the Government were all tinder to verbal pyrotechnics that belied his underlying tolerance and generosity. Yet, although in intellectual argument as fearlessly resolute as he had been physically when he parachuted into France as a medical orderly on D-Day, when it came to plans for his own future with Meg, Jake proved to be far more cautious than Peter had been with me.

Different again from the lives of Meg and me was the one Pluckie – that other close friend of earlier years – had established for herself. She had managed to keep closer to the artistic style of life that she and I had so passionately wished for in our boring days in the City, and, because I was embroiled in mothering and she was not, once I had arrived in Hackney we kept in touch more often by letters than meetings. Earning her living as a teacher in the East End during the week, Pluckie continued to follow her artistic interests at weekends and married a Canadian artist named Alexander soon after they had met on one of her frequent visits to the National Gallery.

For the times, Pluckie's was a very unconventional marriage, in which she continued to teach and provide the household income, while Alexander worked at his paintings. At the end of each day after their supper had been cooked and eaten, Pluckie took off her clothes and became Alexander's unpaid model. In the long holidays they were able to share the joys of Europe's art galleries and return home with their sketch-books full. It was a style of life that suited them both and, successful and fulfilled in her own career, Pluckie was content to be the main support of her artist husband, despite his lack of great success (or at least great recognition). She also came to enjoy the love of generations of children she herself inspired, and she never had the time or the inclination to regret having none of her own.

Just as all marriages make new partnerships, they also break up old friendships. For many years we lost touch with my friends Pat and Frank (shamefully neglecting to repay £20 – a tidy sum then – that they had lent us in the early months of our marriage), and although we lived lesss than a mile away from Peter's old friend Derek Pont and his wife Rita we were glad to sever that link and drift apart from them. The stresses that sharing the same house had imposed on all of us had left too deep a mark – especially on Peter, who remained strongly and untypically antagonistic towards Rita. In quite different circumstances another friend who was soon to disappear into the past was Ann Horton. She had decided to find a new job – and perhaps a new husband – in a country where prospects for both were likely to be better, and happily turned out to be. In the sunset days of the British Empire she went to work as a hospital social worker in a hospital in Malaya, met and married a young English rubber planter not long after, and started a family as soon as she could. Before she went away she asked Peter if he would take over the task of selling her little MG car, which she said we could use ourselves until he found a good buyer.

Having a car, even though only on loan, was still a luxury in the 1950s. To me it was one of the brighter signs that the future might not continue to be as hard as it had been. It meant that at least at weekends we could escape whenever we felt like it to stay with Ben at Great Chesterford, whose country charms I was once again able to appreciate. We could also get over for Sunday dinner at Lee far more easily – and in far less time – than by bus or train.

More excitingly, we could get out to meet the new friends Peter was making in the Labour Party, and about whom I had heard so much. Some of these, like Denis Healey and Peter Shore, who were to become important political figures in the years ahead, were never more than passing acquaintances I knew briefly, or listened to with awe at parties. But amongst those who became a friend was Wilfred Fienburgh, the man who had first guided Peter when he took on *Talking Points* at the Labour Party. The son of a Bradford millworker and a mother who was an active member (and councillor) in the local Labour Party, he had left school early, moving from one unskilled job to another, and was sometimes unemployed. As with so many others, it was the war that first gave him the chance to show his abilities. Called up in 1940, he was commissioned in the Rifle Brigade before the year was out. During the war he was wounded in Normandy, awarded the MBE, and quickly rose to the rank of major on the General Staff. Darkly handsome with an alert and ever-watchful look in his fine brown eyes, he was a man who both attracted and loved women – usually more for their physical charms than their intellectual abilities. Drivingly ambitious, he left the Labour Party (in which for a short while he had stepped into Michael Young's job as Research Secretary) to become Member of Parliament for North Islington. Quickly involved in the political issues and intrigues of the day, his own ambitions were predominant, as Herbert Morrison found at the 1952 Labour Party conference, which Peter also attended in his offical capacity as a research assistant, and where Wilfred, to promote his own career, made a Bevanite attack on Morrison – the man who had earlier befriended and encouraged him.

This, however, was not the Wilfred that I came to know at weekends when, in the comfort of his home, and in the midst of his family and friends, he put his ambitions aside. Sprawled out in an armchair, completely idle and relaxed (apart from the ever-vigilant brown eyes), he was transformed into a warm and entertaining host. Yet what had promised to be a brilliant career was to be tragically cut short in 1958 by his death following a car accident. At the age of only thirty-eight, he left behind a desolate widow and four young children, and one novel, *No Love for Johnnie*, to achieve something of the wider recognition and fame that death had snatched from him. Partly autobiographical, and perhaps a cynical self-portrait of his own future career had he lived, it was published posthumously in 1959 and subsequently made into a successful feature film.

To Peter (and to me), the man who was to become of

greatest importance to us was the one who had opened the way to a new career in research for Peter. First as colleague and later as friend, it was with Michael Young that our lives were destined to be most enduringly entwined. Long before we had met I had heard much about him from Peter that impressed me. A product of the progressive Dartington Hall School and the London School of Economics, by his early twenties he was already a director of the prestigious research organization, Political and Economic Planning. A man of ideas (too many, it was sometimes believed by his hard-pressed staff), his charm and persistence made it hard for anyone to resist his demands, not least because of the confidence he inspired and the high standards he rigorously imposed on himself and expected in almost equal measure from others. His vitality and zeal seemed even more amazing in view of the fact that he suffered from recurrent attacks of asthma and lung infections arising from it. These severe bouts of illness and semi-invalidity could sometimes immobilize him physically for weeks. Yet they seldom stopped him from carrying on working – as Peter found out when called on, not always at convenient times, to go to Michael's home (or sometimes hospital room) to discuss his latest ideas for a new policy paper, or the revision of an older one, or some other always urgent proposal.

After the impression I had formed from Peter's reports, my first sight of this remarkable man was a great disappointment. It was at the flat in Westminster Bridge Road of a another Labour Party colleague, a woman who later married a baronet. She was from Lancashire and enjoyed my amazement at finding beetroot in the hot-pot she served up. She assured me it was the traditional ingredient of the dish where she came from. Soon after Peter and I arrived and entered the crowded, smoke-filled room, Peter pointed Michael out to me. Tall and hollow-chested, bony-limbed and flaxen-haired, with clean-cut jaw, pale-blue eyes and a pale, damp face, he seemed as he stood there to be oblivious to his surroundings. I could see that he was quite good-looking, or that he would have been had his mouth not looked like a great red cavern out of which was coming, not singing – or even bellowing – but an outlandish baying sound. He was roaring drunk.

It was all very different from the person I came to meet later. Although only seven or eight years older than we were, to me he seemed wiser, more experienced and far more mature. This first impression was no doubt based on my own expections of how a head of a department should be; but it soon became clear that the superior status I had assigned to Michael was not what he expected or wanted. (Nor has his attitude changed throughout his influential career and later transmogrification as Lord Young of Dartington.) Diffident and reserved to the point of inhibition when talking about himself, he showed a keen interest in everything around him (including people) that was at once striking and – as I soon found – flattering. It was wonderful to find that with Michael my opinions on hospitals, or day care, or life in Hackney were listened to with, if anything, even more respect than when I expounded them to Peter – which was not so surprising because he, as my spouse, had no doubt heard them only too often.

Some time afterwards, Peter brought home a draft of a new report Michael was working on about changes during the century in working-class family life. While Peter was at the Labour Party annual conference I decamped to Lee to stay. It was from there that, inspired by Michael's report, I wrote to Peter a day or two later:

> I've been 'interviewing' Mum and Dad about their origins and forebears. I'm going to write it up for Michael – social mobility of a working class family. Like all these things, it's a fascinating story, even though one of millions no doubt. Mum and Dad were so delighted to find such interest in them and their families that they got in a pound's worth of bottled beer and decided to stay at home for the evening! What a treasure of the past the human mind holds. What amazes me is the *generalness* of this earlier enthusiasm for 'education' as *the* means to 'bettering yourself'. Grandad Noble taught himself to spell by memorizing words on hoardings and repeating them until he knew them. As I remember him he was an avid reader, getting through several books a week in his long retirement.

When I returned to Hackney, I typed out what I had found out and sent the result to Michael. A few days later a card arrived. It said: 'It is one of the most interesting things I've read for quite a time. Can I incorporate some of it in my report?' It was a new boost to my morale.

18
Moving On

A decent interval of about two years after getting married Meg had her first baby, a girl called Janet. By then, Jake had begun his career as a teacher of English, working in one of the new comprehensive schools, and they had moved into a small flat – the top floor of a semi in Ilford. I don't know if Meg's pregnancy was as well organized as the rest of the plans she and Jake had made. Intimate friends though we were, in those days Meg and I were reticent with each other about our sex lives.

My own second pregnancy was just as unpremeditated as the first had been. I had not only given up Marie Stopes and condoms (family planning clinics, and perhaps condoms too, have improved since then) but rejected the Dutch cap with which my practical and competent friend Daphne had arranged for a health visitor to fit me privately after Lewis was born. It was shaped like a doll's bowler-hat, with a hard rim of black rubber. When I put it in I felt like a stuffed chicken, and when I took it out, since we had no bathroom, the only place the thing could be washed was under the kitchen tap. Back in its little cardboard box it was almost as new when I threw it out a year or two later as when I had brought it home. With the Pill not yet on offer, we turned to the 'safe period', which served to add the dangerous thrill of Russian roulette to our unabated passion that neither my discontents nor tiring days and disturbed nights had managed to quell. It seemed as if the irresistible joys of love-making were always more important at the time than the risk of getting pregnant again.

One of the stories that I had got from Mum as a result of my new interest in the family history was about her own mother. Granny Mann (as she was known to me and my brothers, to distinguish her from Dad's mother, whom we called Gran) had given birth to eleven children. 'Never a year went by without she had one in her arms and one in her stomach. That's what she used to say. And that's how it is for some women,' Mum told me. Lewis was already a running, jumping, talking boy not a babe in arms but, pregnant again as I was, there was an unnerving note of fatalism in Mum's words that made me uneasy.

I had always believed that I loved children and that I wanted – one day – to have some of my own. Once actually launched into motherhood I had found that it was much harder than I had realized to combine it with other things I wanted. Or perhaps it would be more accurate to say that I had rejected the idea that motherhood could mean being tied full-time to hearth and home. Unluckily, the type of career I had chosen to follow, and the climate of the times, were not on my side. Nor were the protective maternal feelings that seemed to come with motherhood, and in the same flooding excess as the milk in my breasts.

The psychological theories I had absorbed during my training for social work (and which under the influence of Dr John Bowlby were becoming increasingly fashionable) had convinced me of the primary need of babies and young children for a round-the-clock close bond with their mothers. During the war, mothers of young children had been urged to return to work to help the war effort; but very soon after it had ended, the message had changed. As mothers were encouraged to give up work and go back to their homes (and after the years of separation many were delighted to do so as their menfolk were demobbed and came home), the crèches and day nurseries set up during the war to care for women's babies and toddlers had closed down.

Bedevilled by fears of the emotional damage leaving Lewis might inflict, plus the practical difficulties of finding acceptable care for him, I felt I had to abandon hope of a quick return to work even before I found myself pregnant again. If I were to come to terms with what had seemed like the conflicting needs of self-fulfilment and full-time motherhood, I had to find some other way. In the evenings, with no television then to distract one, I began to review books on social welfare subjects for *Socialist Commentary*, the journal of a small independent group of Socialists to which Peter and I belonged.

Then one day in the last months of my second pregnancy, I wrote a letter to *The Times*. It was a contribution to correspondence that had been going on for days on the subject on which I felt I was becoming so expert – the day care of young children. It was an exciting moment when Peter raced up the stairs early one morning, waving *The Times* before him and saying, 'It's in. Your letter's in!' The correspondence continued and, a week or so later, another letter arrived, inviting me to a meeting of all those who had contributed to it.

I set off on my way to the meeting in one of the familiar Bloomsbury squares in a mood of agreeable anticipation, but very aware that attending a meeting in my advanced state of pregnancy was not at all usual. Dressed in a tentlike coat of green and brown tweed that could not conceal my bulging outline, I was ushered upstairs and into a fine room overlooking the square. There, I found myself facing a bevy of women seated around a long table, at the head of which sat the chairwoman, Lady Allen of Hurtwood, well known for her interest in play facilities for children. 'Oh, Mrs Willmott,' exclaimed one of the women who had rushed over to greet me, 'we have all been so curious to meet you – for we couldn't help wondering who could be writing to *The Times* from *Hackney*.' It was if I had gatecrashed a club.

Happily, my second experience of childbirth – which was imminent – did not end in the traumatic way that the first had done. Although I was considered to be unsuitable for the home confinement I desperately wanted, an enlightened woman doctor at the local clinic had decided to agree to it. 'You might do better at home, and if it does go wrong again we can always get the emergency service out to whip you into hospital,' she said. When the time came, I moved into Meg's room and had a cheery young midwife, who said 'Call me Bunty' and who was delighted to find that Peter wanted to be with me and to do all he could to help her.

'It's another boy, darling,' he said, his voice trembling with relief and emotion when the baby slithered out just as dawn was breaking on a fine May morning. Cleaned up, and with just a hint of a gold fuzz on his head, baby Mikey seemed to me to have a kind of pearly glow when I gazed down at him sleeping peacefully beside my bed in the cradle that Dad had created out of an old beer-barrel cover. Turned upside, and slung like a hammock on a simple wood frame, it looked pretty with the fine frilly cover I had made for it out of the parachute nylon of my honeymoon nightie and trimmed with blue ribbon.

By the time Peter had brought Lewis down to see his brother I felt fine, but as they came through the door I was struck by the contrast between the beauty and bloom of my first-born, with his mop of hair, violet eyes and face rosy from sleep, and Peter's pallor and exhaustion. 'It looks as if you should be in bed, not me,' I said, half jokingly. A day or two later when the midwife came and saw me sitting up in bed feeding the baby, she said, 'You look the picture of happy motherhood.' Well, I thought, you're closer to the truth than was that arrogant consultant at St Thomas's.

Perhaps it was a reflection of my returning confidence that I gave the green and brown tent coat to Mum and replaced it with a smart new one. It came from Jaeger's. Shopping there had until then been beyond my means, but this one was affordable because it was in the Government's utility range. Made from a slightly fluffy blankety material of bright mustard yellow, it was in the new softer style with dropped shoulders. When I went out in it I felt that I was not only brightening myself up, but the grey streets of Hackney as well. I don't think the new pram we brought for the baby could have been so utility, and my pleasure in that faded quickly when I found how heavy and difficult its smart shiny chromium trimmings made humping it up and down the front steps to the hall.

At the Labour Party, Peter's work had changed and developed. He had moved on to become the research department's policy expert on agriculture and food. As secretary to the

National Executive Committee's subcommittee (chaired by
the brilliant but flawed George Brown, with whose rightish-
wing views Peter was by then broadly in sympathy), he had
the satisfaction of being close to big political events and key
politicians, and the pleasure of strolling across to the Palace
of Westminster for briefings, committee meetings and Commons debates.

It had not taken long for Peter to realize that he, like
most of his colleagues at Transport House, operated at several levels. They produced propaganda, but at the same time
knew that was what it was. They were not blinded to the
defects of nationalization, nor did they believe, after the
Conservatives became the Government, that Tory ministers
were evil or dishonest men. But at another level they were
still strongly pro-Labour, still Socialists who believed that a
Labour Government was better than a Conservative one for
Britain and for the great majority of her people, particularly
the poor and low-paid.

Working at the Labour Party had more than compensated
Peter for what he had missed at university, but by the time
three years had gone by his enthusiasm had begun to wane.
Through many discussions with Michael Young, he had become more and more aware of the weaknesses in policies
that so often failed to take into account the wants and needs
of those – usually families – they were meant to help.

We had been in Hackney for almost exactly four years. During that time we had taken Lewis to see the wonders of the
Festival of Britain (at an age when he was too young to
remember it afterwards). We had seen the coronation of the
young Queen Elizabeth on the Movietone News at the cinema.
I had wheeled Mikey in his chromium-bright pram and, with
Lewis chattering away by my side, stood in the heat and
dust in busy Mare Street with other, mainly young mothers
and their children waiting for the same young Queen to drive
by. For her it was the shining beginning of her reign, but I had
still another year to wait before what had sometimes seemed
the bleakest four years of my life were to come to an end.

The 3rd of July 1954 was the memorable day on which I

tore up our ration books, the Conservative Government having finally brought rationing to an end. It was also the day
we left Hackney and moved a mile down the road to our
new home in Bethnal Green. We had the attic flat above
what was about to become the office of the Institute of
Community Studies in which Michael Young, Peter and another
Peter, Peter Townsend (soon to be followed by a third –
Peter Marris), planned to pioneer a new style of sociological
research. It meant surveys and interviews with Bethnal Greeners
about their housing dreams and family life, which were to
lead to an original form of sociological reporting. Dry statis-
tics were to be brought to life by the human warmth of
personal experience in reports that ordinary readers could enjoy
as much as, if not more than, the traditional academic audience.

Our new home was in a tall, beautiful Queen Anne house of
red brick that looked out on to a green square. Bordered on
one side by the long side-wall, with its Victorian decorative
friezes, of the Bethnal Green Museum (an annex of the Vic-
toria and Albert), on the other by the fine white walls of a
Hawksmoor church, and edged by great plane trees, this former
village green on which sheep had grazed was now a public
open space with footpaths and flower-beds interspersing well-
mown grass.

At the top of the impressive oak stairway, smaller stairs led
up to the attic flat we inhabited. The ancient and uneven
oak floor-boards were embellished with red needlecord car-
peting. We had not only our own bathroom but part central
heating, hot and cold water in the kitchen and even a fridge.
The long, low rooms had sloping ceilings and dormer windows which at the front looked on to the square, and at the
back on to a small leather factory, and beyond it to the high,
grim school building in which Lewis, to his dismay, was soon
to find himself doomed to daily incarceration.

Sunday, 29 August
Tonight, one thought obsesses me – that my Lewis is off
to school tomorrow, now being a 'big boy' of five years
old. I am terrified, yet also pleased. Terrified in case the

world buffets Lewis unkindly. Pleased because from now on I have the benefit of a 'governess' – State provided. Lewis is no longer mine alone from morn until night (and Mikey won't be either when he begins nursery school next year). Odd to think that thirty-odd other mothers in nearby Bethnal Green are getting ready tonight to hand over *their* little darlings – all as convinced as I am about Lewis that he or she is going to delight, astonish and generally stand out to the teacher. She no doubt awaits a new batch of the old stuff, familiar as copper coins and as similar! But I expect I am the only mother in Bethnal Green who is recording the beginning of term for the five-year-olds of September '54.

I was not to know then how much not only my life but everyone's was to change as full employment and the buoyant years of the 1960s drew closer. What I did sense was that the move to our attic eyrie, although this was hardly palatial, heralded better times ahead. 'Perhaps you'll get yourselves some decent furniture now,' Mum said pointedly when she made her first visit to see us in our new surroundings. I knew what she meant – a three-piece suite and a dining-table with matching chairs.